THE PROFITABLE BUILDER'S PLAYBOOK

The Step-by-Step Guide to Building a Profitable Residential Construction Business That Gives You True Wealth—BOTH More Money and More Time

MARTI AMOS

www.theprofessionalbuilder.com

TPB THE
PROFESSIONAL
BUILDER

UNLOCK YOUR

$3,000

BUILDER BONUS PACK

Unlock the tools, done-for-you templates and calculators that go with the book.
Scan this code to get instant access to all of your tools.

SCAN ME

WHAT'S INCLUDED

Planning & Strategy Tools

- The Builders Roadmap
- The Business Maturity Plan Worksheet
- The 4 Levers of Profit Calculator

Pricing & Margin Tools

- The Professional Builders Rate (PBR) Calculator
- The High-Converting Quote Template
- The Guarantee Template

Systems & Team Tools

- The Team Gold Meeting Framework
- The Hiring Guide
- The Rules of the Game

These bonuses are only available to verified buyers of The Profitable Builder's Playbook.

Published by Prominence Publishing.

ISBN: 978-1-990830-61-7

TABLE OF CONTENTS

DEDICATION

To my wife, Kelly, for encouraging me to pursue all of my goals and dreams. I love sharing my life with you.

To my boys Ashton and Zak, it's a pleasure to see you grow and develop into fine young men, try new things, and live life to the fullest.

To Mum and Dad, for being great role models and providing me with a great work ethos and "can-do" attitude.

ACKNOWLEDGEMENTS

To my amazing team at The Professional Builder for giving your all, levelling up in all ways, and always striving to become the best version of yourselves.

Owen, you are a rockstar. It's great to be on this journey together with you.

Lucy (my office wife), you make my life easier, better, and more productive (and fun).

Vinnie, Jeremy, James, Brynn, Fher, Lorence, Miriam, Randy, Kevin, Cole, Carla, Mathew BG, Maricel, and Christine, you guys rock!

Sandi, great work editing down 300+ pages, and Claire for putting the finishing touches on the manuscript and turning my Doctor's scrawl into English.

All of our members over the last 21+ years on a journey to level up their business and get better every day in every way.

This book and these resources are for you.

Here's to your success!

Marti Amos

INTRODUCTION
CHAPTER SUMMARY

Being a great builder and building a great business require two different skill sets, which you can learn if you have the desire.

- Build a great business on more than just referrals ('hope' marketing).

- Work harder on smarter things.

- Your business should give you both more money AND more time = freedom.

- Systems run the business and we hire and train people to run these systems.

- Numbers are the language of business; focus on the key numbers that will drive more profit.

- To implement the strategies in this book, scan the QR code so you can access the plug-and-play resources featured at the end of each chapter.

INTRODUCTION

In my 21 years of coaching construction companies, I have found that most building company owners are great at the construction side and do great work. In fact, my coaching company has now had over 87 of our members win House of the Year Awards since the business started in 2004. This being said, we've found that accolades don't always go hand in hand with business success and wealth.

Quite often, we meet people who are great at the construction side but need help growing their business for the long term. This is because building owners were all sold a big, fat lie:

If you do great work and rely on word of mouth, things will work out. If you just work long enough and hard enough, eventually, it will all pay off, and you'll have the business of your dreams.

Old school building company owners used to be able to do well by just doing great builds, working hard, and relying on referrals to keep them going. This just doesn't work anymore.

PROFITABLE BUILDING GOES BEYOND REFERRALS

Referrals are great, but you can't rely upon them to come when you need them to. Hope is not a strategy. The truth is, there's no way to predict consistent referrals. You can't control what other people do. We fixed this problem with our TPB 1% Referrals System. Besides, referrals are the cream on top, not the whole cake. You need to install a marketing machine to consistently bring in the right type of projects.

PROFITABLE BUILDING GOES BEYOND EFFORT

I love building company owners because of their tendency toward a great work ethic. They understand the value of effort, but it can easily get out of hand in the name of "growth."

They burn the candle at both ends! They work twelve-hour days, price projects at night, scheduling guys on Sundays, constantly obsess over materials, and are always on call. Neglecting yourself and pushing harder is not just unfeasible — it's ludicrous and, unfortunately, it's an all-too-common trend.

Owners often go years without time off and when they do get time off, they spend it worrying about what's happening on site while they are away. Even when they are home at night with the family, they aren't really present because they are thinking about work 24/7.

Will the concrete show up on time tomorrow?

When will that cladding be in stock?

How much should I be paying my foreman, my carpenters, my apprentice?

Many builders don't understand their true costs and margins and have no strong business differentiation, so it can feel like they are in a race to the bottom, competing on price—all whilst being price-checked by clients against other builders.

The fact is a lot of building company owners make up for a lack of business acumen with sheer effort and brute force. They hold on for dear life, hoping it all works out and that there's enough money to pay the guys their wages, order materials, and pay the merchant. And then taxes hit, which leads to overwhelm, stress, sleepless nights, and anxiety (again, hope is not a strategy).

I know. I've been there.

I know how it feels to lie awake in bed at night wondering how to pay the wages, pay the bills, with the weight of the world (and my team) all on my shoulders. A lot of people depended on me, and I was fighting a losing battle—one step forward, two steps back. It was a dark time in my life, and I don't want anyone else to feel like I did if I can help them avoid it.

It's no wonder the construction sector has one of the highest (if not the highest, in some countries) suicide rates and is fraught with builders struggling with mental illness. It kills me to see building company owners struggling because there's a better way.

THE GOOD NEWS

There is a proven process to go from struggle street to a building business that reaps true wealth. It's what my coaching company has been developing over the last 21 years. We've tested and tried over 400 strategies for marketing, sales, pricing, cash flow, profit, hiring, on-site systems, admin, team, and leadership.

As of 2024, my company, The Professional Builder (TPB), has helped over 2500+ residential construction companies turn themselves around and become well-systemised and profitable. Our community throughout the USA, Canada, the UK, Australia, and New Zealand is responsible for over $7 billion in revenue and $1.5 billion in gross profit, and growing daily.

> *"It's not about working harder or working smarter. What's important is working harder on smarter things."*
>
> –Zane Beckett, ZB Homes, winner of the Deloitte Fast 50[1]

We've helped building company owners regain control over their time, make more money, and, best of all, regain their passion and enjoyment for

---

[1] Fastest-growing company in New Zealand in 2017. This was the first time a construction company had won this in 50 years.

their business. That's why most of us got into business in the first place: to build a better life, make an impact, and build something we can be proud of.

This is what Alvin Chisnall, who works in remodels and renovations, had to say:

> *"We have been in Europe about one week of our six-week holiday...the good thing is, while I have been away, my staff have signed up one job and are negotiating the floor covering on a second job."*

THE BUILDER'S ROADMAP

What you hold in your hands is the culmination of all my experience working with residential construction companies and franchises of various types and different markets—from rural areas and small towns to big cities, from poor to affluent. We've made truckloads of mistakes along the way and refined our process to a scalable, sustainable system that anyone who is willing to put in the work can implement.

Our system is called the Builder's Roadmap, which we've refined and battle-tested in the trenches day to day with the top 5% of residential construction companies. It's simple but not easy (just like a diet) and different than you might expect.

More Money + More Time = Freedom

In this book, you will learn how to:

- Get paid what you are worth.
- Make more profit per job.
- Systemise your business and lead your team.
- Manage and lead your business by the numbers.
- Buy back your time so you can work on the business rather than in it.

The Profitable Builder's Playbook is the step-by-step playbook every residential construction business owner should use to fast-track their results. You will achieve more in the next 12 months using the strategies in this book than you could by trying to figure it all out on your own over the next 5 years. At the end of each chapter, you'll have the tools you need to assess the progress of your business every 90 days to ensure you're always on the right track to creating the company that you know is possible with the right strategies.

SYSTEMS WILL SET YOU FREE

Even if you only implement one system a week, it's going to make a massive difference in 90 days, let alone where you could be in 12 months' time.

Think about it like this: If someone else has succeeded at what you want to improve upon (stepped outside their comfort zone, hired an estimator to price their projects, hired an office manager, or started to charge for quotes), then you can do it as well. There's a solution out there for the exact problem that you're going through right now. Someone has gone through the same problem, figured it out, and built a repeatable system to get the same or a similar result that you want.

NUMBERS WILL ALSO SET YOU FREE

What sets this book apart is that it will help you understand the key numbers that drive profit and where to focus your energy for maximum profit.

Building a successful company has three key components:

1. Attract and convert your ideal prospects into a steady stream of projects.

2. Deliver quality jobs with best-practice on-site and office systems for your team to follow.

3. Make sure those jobs deliver great profit and consistent cash flow with the right pricing model so you can grow your business.

Don't let the numbers side of things scare you. If you're not into numbers or business models, that's okay. I'm going to walk you through each concept step-by-step so you can understand them easily and apply the right strategies to improve your business.

One such solution is our Growth Accelerator model. We use it with every residential building company we work with. It's amazing how fast things can improve with this system, just like they did for Michael:

> *"TPB has been a game changer for me. When we came on with TPB, we were at a run rate of $1M-$1.2M a year. We're now looking at busting through $2.8M."*
>
> —Michael P, Texas

I'll explain in more depth later how the machine works and break it down for you step by step, and also show you how to build a high-performing team and a culture of accountability.

HOW DOES THIS HELP YOU?

If you take some time out to really study this book and actually IMPLEMENT even a few of its strategies, you will add more revenue to your company and make more profit. I promise you the results you are seeking from your business are found in this book, but it's on you to take the principles you learn here and actually EXECUTE them. Here are some words from our members that show just some of the results our TPB community has achieved:

"Friday win! Hired two new qualified carpenters. Just won a $1.8m house. Workload is booked for 17 staff for 12 months. Holy! Thanks TPB."

—Lain H, Fairlie

"Win for the week/month was signing up a $250,000 extension on a Cost plus 23% basis! It's nice to have a couple of Cost Plus jobs in the pipeline as this takes a lot of pressure off while we continue to implement more of the TPB strategies and get some systems up and running."

—Josh B, Wellington

"We just expanded our team. Hired an apprentice and Foreman so our team is now a total of 6. We've also got another builder who we're looking to hire, too. Now Korey can get off the tools very soon and can focus on growing the business! We're stoked!"

—Nikki G, Aukland

"Day 11 of 75 Hard. Daily morning routine in place due to 75 Hard. Lightest weight I've been in 16 years. Final design meeting and into paid estimate for next residential project... value around $1,100,000. Estimate charge is $3,300 + QS costs on top. Finally worked out FB forms for lead ad. Thanks TPB... you guys are awesome and we are always grateful for the partnership we have found in y'all."

—Michael S, Queensland

I can make such a bold promise because most of the construction companies we have worked with have only implemented about one-third of the techniques I'm sharing with you. Even without using all our principles, they have seen an increase in top-line revenue growth (and bottom-line profit) — plus, they've regained their time, sanity, and family.

WHAT'S IN IT FOR ME?

One word: TRUST. I'd like to earn yours by helping you get results. Try just a couple of tactics from the book and see them work. Make more money, and then try some more. You'll see your security and peace of mind grow and be proud of the work you put in — but in the right places and at the right times this time around!

Are you ready to see your sites run smoother and your bank account grow?

Let's get to it!

–Marti Amos, Founder, The Professional Builder

ACTION STEPS

- Download the tools in each chapter to fast-track your results: https://profitablebuilderbook.com/resources

- Watch the member results to see what's possible for your business.

Here are 3 ways TPB can help you:

1. Listen to the podcast at https://theprofessionalbuilder.com/podcasts

2. Book a call with one of our coaches to see if we can help you fast-track your goals https://profitablebuilderbook.com/call

3. Check the health of your business here: https://audit.theprofessionalbuilder.com and find out what areas to work on right now for maximum results

Scan the code for all the resources:

PART ONE

THE MINDSET OF A PROFITABLE BUILDER

Along your journey to becoming a profitable business owner, some things are going to be new to you. You're going to have to do a lot of learning. Luckily for you as a business owner in the construction sector, there is a big financial incentive to learn what you need to know to be more profitable. And as I like to say, all learning is, is *earning* with L-plates[1] on it.

Part One of this book is all about how to think, lead, systemise, and interact with your team like a profitable building business owner. The skills you'll acquire from implementing the strategies in this section will reap many rewards for both your business and your personal life. You'll actually enjoy what you do and leave what isn't worth your time or energy behind. Your time and energy are precious resources, only to be used on what will make the most impact on your business and your quality of life. Now, let's get you more money—and more time!

---

[1] In certain countries, L-plates (a square plate with the letter "L" on it) are placed on cars to indicate that a driver is still learning.

CHAPTER 1 – SUMMARY
MINDSET OF A PROFITABLE BUILDER

- To change your results in your business requires doing things differently. Some ideas might be counterintuitive, like "get paid more by doing less" and breaking any self-limiting beliefs that are keeping you in the same situation.

- Focus your efforts on the 80/20 big needle movers for your business.

- Scale the builder's ladder with the right strategies for your revenue size.

- Be x Do = Have. Use the Formula for success to reverse engineer the type of life (and business) you want to have and what you need to do.

- Get clear on the lifestyle you are building: clarity and focus are your superpowers.

- Operate in your zone of genius. Tasks that:
  - Have a big impact
  - You love doing them
  - You are naturally great at them

- Use the fun/skills matrix and freedom finder to get rid of the low level tasks.

- Track your PBR (Professional Builders Rate) to buy back 8 hours per 90 days and get paid more.

- Identify your Stop Doing List to free up time every 90 days.

- Build out your perfect week using the Default Diary to make sure you set yourself up to win the week

GET PAID MORE BY DOING LESS

Work harder on smarter things. Focus on the 80/20

We all need more time. Maybe you want to participate more at your kids' school. Maybe you want to be able to take a week off without thinking about your business 24/7. Or you might want to be like one of our members, Adam, and take two weeks off to go to Europe and have the business run smoothly without you. If any of these goals resonate with you, you've come to the right place. The Builder's Roadmap is all about making sure that you get the systems in place to make your dreams a reality.

These are the same systems all of our members at The Profitable Builder have used to make their dreams come true, like Mark Taylor from Tauranga, New Zealand, who owns MLT Builders Limited:

> *"Before I started with TPB, I was always just chasing the dollar, taking anything that came in because my cash flow was poor. I had no systems in place, and I was just constantly chasing my tail. I had no clue what I was up to, but I thought I knew what I was up to. And then I had these big expectations of, 'This is where I want to be.' But I just couldn't get there. Like, 'What are all these guys around me doing that's different from what I'm doing?' I [knew I was a] good builder, but I didn't know how to climb up. That's why I joined TPB. And now I'm fully booked until next year with margins around 20-25%."*

These systems not only gave him more money, but they also gave him more time:

> "I used to work every day, including weekends. I would come home and do paperwork and payroll, then sleep and repeat. It was wearing me down, and my wife was really worried. I decided I had to make a change. That's another reason why I joined TPB...I took six days completely off the grid and came back to all the sites running on track with no issues. When you put in place the systems TPB provides, it gives you the confidence that the wheels won't fall off the tracks."

I share this with you to encourage you to dream big dreams. You already have the means to make something like this happen for yourself using the assets you've already spent so much blood, sweat, and tears to create. Now it's time for you to work smarter on the right things instead of working harder—and certainly not on the wrong things. With this book, you'll know what isn't worth your time and use what motivates you to keep chipping away at the tasks you need to do to accomplish your dreams.

You may have noticed Mark said he couldn't "climb up." He's referring to the Builder's Ladder that we developed at The Profitable Builder as part of the Builder's Roadmap. To get your time back, instead of staying chained to the builder's hamster wheel, you need to focus on climbing the Builder's Ladder. In other words, your mindset must change from that of a builder to that of a businessman and then to an entrepreneur as you grow.

Before we go into the specifics of focusing on how to climb the Builder's Ladder (which includes getting clear on the roles you need to hire people to fill, systemising the tasks to be done by each person, and knowing how to hire), let's talk about what you want your business to create for you. Your vision will be what's at the top of the ladder—the thing that will keep you focused on climbing—and don't look down!

FROM BUSY BUILDER TO BUSINESS OWNER

Builder's Ladder

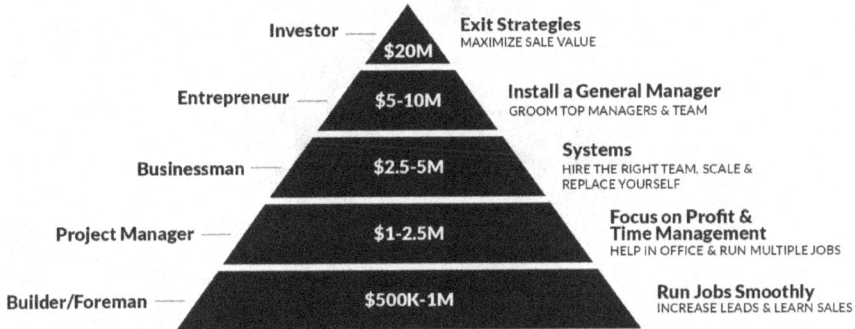

Investor —	$20M	**Exit Strategies** MAXIMIZE SALE VALUE
Entrepreneur —	$5-10M	**Install a General Manager** GROOM TOP MANAGERS & TEAM
Businessman —	$2.5-5M	**Systems** HIRE THE RIGHT TEAM, SCALE & REPLACE YOURSELF
Project Manager —	$1-2.5M	**Focus on Profit & Time Management** HELP IN OFFICE & RUN MULTIPLE JOBS
Builder/Foreman —	$500K-1M	**Run Jobs Smoothly** INCREASE LEADS & LEARN SALES

Critical Success Factors

Systems That Run The Business	Marketing & Sales
	Understand Your Numbers
People That Run The Systems	Deliver a Profitable Project

Let's clarify your why to keep you motivated to change your habits, and you'll learn why it's tempting to go back to your old ways of trying to juggle everything! But this is absolutely the wrong mindset and it will keep you stuck at your current level while you slowly (or not so slowly) burn out.

GETTING CLEAR ON YOUR VISION

Now, what does *your* ideal lifestyle look like? In other words, what do you want to HAVE, who do you want to BE, and what do you need to DO to get there?

1. Leader With a Clear Vision
2. Action Oriented
3. Solution Focused

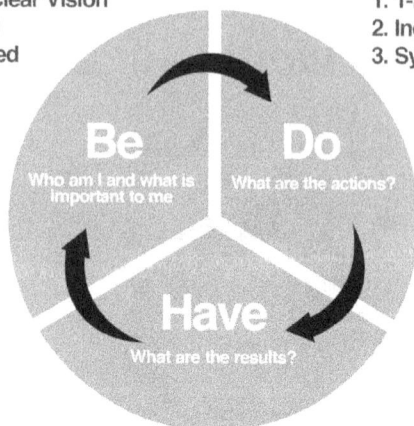

1. 1-Page Business Plan
2. Increase Gross Margin %
3. Systemise the Business

Be
Who am I and what is important to me

Do
What are the actions?

Have
What are the results?

1. Vivid Vision Booklet
2. More Time & More Money
3. Dream Planner

HAVE

What do you want to have in your life in terms of family time, holidays, houses, cars, motorcycles, or toys? Get some photos. Pin those up where you can see them every day. Put them into a vision book so you stay motivated. Change is exciting, but as you set new goals, you'll find it can be difficult to change the way you've always done things. Having a clear vision helps remind you to continue to make the right choices, even when things get tough (as they will when you are growing your business, making changes, and stepping out of your comfort zone).

THE GOAL ACHIEVER PROCESS

We use a four-step process to turn goals into reality. It's called IVVM, which stands for:

1. Idealise:

What do you ideally want your life to look like? Clarity is key here.

2. Visualise:

When the mind has a tangible picture of success, it makes it more concrete and, thus, more achievable. There are actions you can take to create the tangible feeling of what you desire.

Let's say you want to buy a Porsche GT3. You can go to your local Porsche dealer, take it for a drive and take it home. Get a photo of the family in it, get photos of it in your garage, and then chuck that photo up on your wall so you see it every day. This is what I did.

If your goal is to take two weeks off to go to Fiji to scuba dive, then you'll need to make sure you schedule that time out in advance and book the flights and accommodation. You create the vacuum.

Let's say you want to take the family on a vacation to Disneyland. Go and put down a deposit, create the vacuum by booking the time off, share with the family, "Here's where we're going," and get your family involved in your vision boarding process. Here's what my vision board looks like, just to give you some ideas:

3. Verbalise:

Watch the way you speak to yourself and others about your goals. Monitor your self-talk, and verbalise positive things about your goals as much as you possibly can.

4. Materialise:

You can do all the mindset stuff, all the good internal stuff, and you can put it up on the wall and tell everyone about it, but what needs to happen? Action, right? Massive action in the right direction starts with clear goals, a strong motivating reason why, a step-by-step action plan specific to your situation, and goals broken down into achievable milestones.

BE

Ask yourself, *"Who do I need to **BE** to make this a reality? Do I need to be someone who learns more in order to grow my business?"* Maybe you need to be someone who understands numbers more or puts in place better systems onsite and in the office.

DO

Lastly, ask yourself, *"What do I need to **DO** to make this a reality?"* Now, this one is tricky because business owners tend to pile on tasks and never get them all done.

What do you need to do differently to improve your results? Quite often, you don't need the motivation to speed you up. You need education to turn the ship around. What's the 80/20? These are the tasks that would be a game changer for your business.

It's deep, right? It's a write-it-downer. What we're going to do now is create the fuel behind your will to change things about your life. (This is the part I love the most.)

Ask yourself: What do I want my lifestyle to look like?

Take your time to properly write out your ideal lifestyle to manifest it faster. Remember, **will set + skill set + massive action = success.**

Your life's dreams you'd rather be spending time on are your *why* for doing the business in the first place. They will keep you going when things get tough. They will motivate you to make things happen. Getting clear on why you do what you do is integral to the Builder's Roadmap for profit, success, and living a life you're proud of.

> *"Working with Marti helped me achieve the things that I had hoped for. I can renovate my home, plan for holidays, and buy cars. I used to think they were just a dream, but having a profitable business allowed me to have them."*
>
> —Doug G, Sydney

Contrary to popular belief, prioritising what you want to do actually brings in more money. Why is this? Well, doing something you want to be doing makes you more likely to do it—and more likely to do it well—thus making it sustainable. When this concept is applied to the roles you take on in your business—in other words, when you're only doing what is best for you and the business—you will gain the profit you want in order to spend time the way you want to spend it. To make space for the most profitable tasks, let's first remove the things you're currently doing that you could let someone else do and that you are going to stop doing altogether.

LIFESTYLE DREAM BUILDER

These are the life dreams of: Bob the Builder
Chosen on:

The Professional Builder Lifestyle Builder Process

Idealization. Complete these pages making sure you describe your most ideal life. Shoot for the stars and at the very least you'll hit the moon.

HAVE: WE'LL EXPLORE THE PHYSICAL THINGS, TOYS, OR 'STUFF' YOU WANT TO HAVE.

Houses	: How many, where, worth, each one with of beds/baths/other rooms, views, outside etc...
Cars	: Make, model, year, colour, rego plate, interior type and colour.
Boats	: Make, model, feet, colour, interior, no of berths, names, year, Jetski.
Bikes	: Push, motor, road, dirt, rego plates, colour.
Jewellery	: His/hers, watches (make, model, metal/colour stones), necklaces (metal/colour, stones, weight).
Furniture	: Make, model, colour, type, colour, age, antiques, modern, designer, brands.

Electronic Stuff: Stereos, Apple Products, iPhones, 3D Glasses, Google Glasses, Laptops, Games, telescopes, Kitchen, cameras, toys, phones, tools, motorized tools, garden tools, appliances, TV's, cinemas.

Art : Paintings, sculptures, photographs, memorabilia, prints, waterscapes.

Pets : Dogs, cats, birds, guard dogs, fish.

Clothes : Brands, shops you are well known in,

Investments

Properties : Residential, no of and bed/bath, suburbs/areas, wealth wheels, blocks of units, monthly passive, total value per year.

Shares : Options, warrants, futures, equities, managed funds, blue chips, tech/biotech, mining, retail.

Cash : Bank accounts in which countries, how much cash in each?

Businesses : How many, turnover/profits, no of employees, no of offices/stores, industries.

DO: LET'S LOOK AT THE THINGS YOU WANT TO DO, THE PLACES YOU WANT TO GO, AND THE EXPERIENCES YOU WANT TO HAVE IN YOUR LIFE.

Major achievements : Business, family, investing, sports/hobbies

Awards : Which ones, from whom, what for? ...

Donations : Time/money, which charities, functions, amounts?

Kids money : How much, when, what rules?

FIRST THINGS FIRST: INSPECT YOUR DAILY TASKS

What if I told you that in the next 90 days, you could gain a whole day of free time back to be spent as you choose? With The Builder's Roadmap, you will gain some tools that will help you cultivate the right mindset to help you take back 8 hours (one whole work day) in the next 90 days. This process starts with a brain dump of the tasks you do every day.

> *"The biggest change with TPB is buying back my time. I can spend time with my kids, pick them up from school, and go on a vacation with the whole family. I'm able to check in with my operations guy and know everything is running smoothly."*
>
> –Lance I, West Melton

Not all of the tasks you do during the day create value. Think about all the operational aspects that you cover in your business. As you grow your company, you have to elevate your position and decide what you're NOT going to do. From here on out, think like a profitable builder. This means you need to hire new people and decide what tasks they are going to do.

Your Genius Zone

Now, to prepare for this step, list all of the tasks you do on a daily basis, whether that be at home or for your business. Circle all the tasks you're currently doing that

- You hate doing
- Are repeatable
- Are not important for you, the business owner, to be doing

…and this includes your personal stuff at home. Really strive to circle as many as you can (you'll thank me later).

Think about why you don't want to be doing these tasks. They are likely things *within* the business that someone else should be doing so you can focus on building the business.

To go up the Builder's Ladder and go from builder to businessman, you must solve the challenges of getting a smooth running job site so that you are not getting pulled back in to put out the fires. This is why you've got to stay focused on the tasks you're more likely to do—the ones you're more likely to do well. The secret to this focus is incentive, and what's more incentivising than *fun*? (more money springs to mind).

- To enjoy the experience of being a profitable builder, quite frankly, you need to enjoy what you're doing and operate only from your zone of genius. Your zone of genius is where the following three things intersect:

- What you're great at

- What you most enjoy

- What adds the most value to the company

THE PROFESSIONAL BUILDER

Your Zone of Genius

Task	$ Value of Task	Impactful On My Business	My Genius	Love Doing	Who Does The Role Currently and Decision For Future	Time Frame To Complete Change	Actions to Take to Achieve Change	What Effect Will The Change Have On The Business
Estimating and Pricing Jobs	$75	Yes	No	No	Outsourcing	60 Days	Speak to Estimator	Better and more timely estimates and free up my time
Project Scheduling	$100	Yes	Yes	Yes	PM and more delegation by PM to Site Supervisors	60 Days	Construction manager in charge of project scheduling and he will start giving site managers the role and he will review	Empowers the team frees up the PM
Sales and Tender Presentations	$100	Yes	Yes	Yes	Part of My Role	Remain as is	Continue in role until I have a permanent sales person	Creates a better pipeline and growth plan
Variations	$75	Yes	No	No	PM creates and I review	Remain as is	Construction manager in charge of variations on projects	Empowers the team and produces a step-by-step process
Marketing	$100	Yes	Yes	Yes	Part of My Role	Remain as is	Continue in role until I have a permanent marketing person	Long term growth and business IP and presence
Networking with Architects, Designers, Real Estate Agents and Draftsmen	$100	Yes	Yes	Yes	Part of My Role	Remain as is	Continue with this role	Builds pipeline for work
Onboarding new sub contractors	$75	Yes	Yes	Yes	PM and more delegation by PM to Site Supervisors	90 Days	Delegate to my PM	Frees up my time identifies my PM as the person in charge of all aspects on construction. Makes him responsible for who he chooses

For larger views of the tables featured in this book, scan the QR code at the end of each chapter to access a complete list of resources and images.

Finding and operating in your zone of genius is precisely what will make you a truckload more money. We have a system whereby you can spend more time with family, have fun, work on your fitness, or do whatever it is you want to do. Our system is called **The Fun/Skills Matrix**—and it will massively increase your productivity.

So, how does the Fun/Skills Matrix work? Well, the first key thing is to recognise that not everything you do during the week has the same value. Twenty percent of the things you do are going to be the $1,000-$2,000 an hour tasks, and some of the things you might be currently doing *within the business* are the $30 an hour tasks.

So, get out that list you made when inspecting your daily tasks. We already looked at the ones you shouldn't be doing, so let's now identify the ones you do. These will be the 20% of activities that you do during the week that produce 80% of the results. Once you get clear on what these are, spend more time in this zone doing that 20%.

You also need to look at what you are doing that is low-fun and low-skill to help you identify which tasks can be immediately delegated.

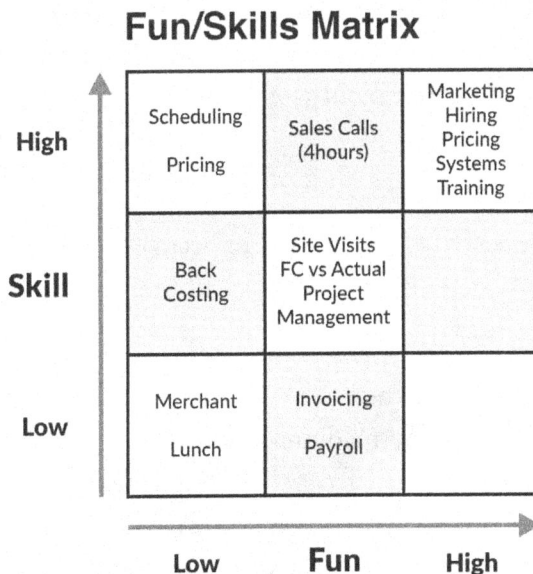

Fun/Skills Matrix

	Low Fun	Fun	High Fun
High Skill	Scheduling Pricing	Sales Calls (4hours)	Marketing Hiring Pricing Systems Training
Skill	Back Costing	Site Visits FC vs Actual Project Management	
Low Skill	Merchant Lunch	Invoicing Payroll	

Something like going to the merchant might be low fun and low skill. Doing the payroll? Maybe it sucks. Maybe you don't like it. Maybe site setup sucks. Anyone can do that. So, you want to be thinking, "Could someone else do this? Am I the only person who can do this in the business? Is this the best use of my time?"

Next, work out what is medium-skill, but may be low fun. This might include tasks like invoicing.

And then, what are the high-skill/high-fun tasks for you? This is where you'll find the tasks that have the most value, the ones that carry the most weight. This is the "working *ON* instead of *IN* the business." Putting systems in place. Signing deals with clients. Marketing. What are the $1,000-an-hour tasks that make a massive difference in your business?

Next, alongside each task, write down how many hours you spend doing it. Did you spend four hours going to the merchant? Two hours doing payroll, chasing the guys for their timesheets? Maybe you spent two hours on site setup.

> "One of the biggest things I learned from TPB was to have a clear team structure and management. I'm not looking at paperwork or messaging clients back and forth. When there are problems, my team can fix them without getting me involved."
>
> —Jon F, Texas

Fill in all your weekly tasks into their respective categories based on how you feel about each task and the level of specialised skill required to complete it.

Once you've gotten rid of the low-skill/low-fun (and thus low value) stuff, move on to delegating the medium-skill/medium-fun stuff. This is how you go about gradually but effectively systemizing your business, making sure that you're working on the high-dollar-value tasks: the 20% that generate 80% of your results each week. Have a crack at it. It'll change your life. Do this every 90 days and watch your business grow and buy back your time and sanity.

> *"Thanks to Marti and TPB team, I've stepped fully out of project management. Now I'm focused on having a helicopter view of my business. I'm going to reward myself with a trip to South Africa and meet my partner's parents."*
>
> —Russell C, Auckland

HOW TO GET TO THE $1,000-AN-HOUR TASKS

To understand the power of doing less in your business and simultaneously making more money, let's take a second to find out how much you currently make per hour based on your salary and profit. Next, we will calculate how much you would make when taking back 8 hours a week of your time at first. This calculation is called your **Professional Builder's Rate (PBR)**.

Knowing your PBR (essentially, what you're worth) will help you prioritise certain tasks over others based on how much they pay. As a profitable builder, when faced with a task, you want to be constantly asking yourself, "Does this task pay below my desired PBR?" But before you get to your desired PBR, let's calculate what you currently make, so we can focus on increasing your PBR, so you get paid what you are worth.

> *"My biggest mindset shift with TPB was letting go and stopping thinking I could do everything myself. Other people would do as good, if not a better job at many things than I did."*
>
> —Doug W, Neutral Bay

WHAT'S YOUR CURRENT PROFESSIONAL BUILDER'S RATE (PBR)?

MY NUMBERS	NOW	90 DAYS	12 MONTHS
SALARY	$70K	$70K	$100K
COMPANY PROFITS	$70K	$70K	$150K
TOTAL	$140K	$140K	$250K
WEEKLY (50X WEEKS)/50	$2800	$2800	$5000
HOURS PER WEEK	60	50	40
PBR/HR	$47	$56	$125

Your Professional Builder's Rate (PBR) is an equation that shows you your hourly rate as the business owner and can help determine just how much more you would be making if you worked less, whilst installing the right systems.

Let's say you're currently working 60 hours a week and want to regain two more nights—or perhaps even Saturday or Sunday. Your goal within the next 90 days could be to get down to working 50 hours a week.

(Total salary + company profits) ÷ 50 weeks ÷ # of weekly work hours = your PBR

Using the example of working 60 hours a week, let's say your total salary plus your company profits added up to $140,000, and you divide that by 50 weeks (52 weeks in a year minus two weeks you might take off), it would be $2,800 that you make per week. Then, divide that number by the 60 hours you currently work, and your current PBR would be $46.66 per hour.

$140,000 ÷ 50 weeks ÷ 60 hours= $46.66

Now, What's Your Desired PBR?

If you instead divide the $2,800 by your desired work hours of 50 a week (10 less than before), you will have raised your hourly rate to $56.

$140,000 ÷ 50 weeks ÷ 50 hours= $56

In this example, by working less, your hourly rate goes from roughly $47 to $56 an hour! You would then repeat this calculation every month to make sure you're on track, and every 90 days, work to free up more of your time as you put systems in place and train your team by relinquishing the lower level tasks from your work week.

Most people only focus on making more money, not freeing up their time or reducing their stress, which are the two key components of becoming a profitable builder. They create a hell for themselves this way—a prison—whereby they're working all hours of the week and they don't have a plan on how to grow a business that works for them. I want to show you how to run a business that works for *you*. Let's find your freedom using your desired hourly rate with a very useful tool we at The Professional Builder call the Freedom Finder.

THE FREEDOM FINDER

Now that you've identified the tasks you want to stop doing, you're inevitably going to be moving away from the lower dollar-per-hour tasks. The Freedom Finder will help you identify what those tasks are and help you move in the direction of the $100-an-hour tasks, and then to the $1,000-an-hour tasks.

Task List

Less than $50/hour	Less than $100/hour	Over $100/Hour	$1,000 per hour
Daily Site Visits	Client Updates	TPB Training	Planning and organizing your day
Weekly Toolbox Meetings	Invoicing	Lead Generation	Negotiating with a hot prospect
Daily Stand Ups	Change Orders	Quote Presentations	Sleep & Relaxation
Material Orders	Financial Tracking	Training	Delegating complex tasks
Material Pick Ups	Subcontractor Scheduling	Site Meetings (sales)	Negotiating with suppliers
On the tools	Quality Control	Hiring A+ Staff	Back costing each job in real time
Site Prep	Estimating	Leading Management Meetings	Pricing process improvements
Site Clean Up	Debtor Management		Building and testing systems/machines
Posting on Socials	Back Costing		Exercise
Emails			Hanging out with smart people on the same journey
Purchase Orders			Meditation
Managing Time Sheets			Distribution of marketing content
Doing admin			Labour Tracking review
Payroll			Variations & Tracking Processes
			Chasing up contractors who are letting you down
			Quote brief & presentation
			Improving Hiring Process
			Upgrading Info Pack

■▬ Architectural Builders ···

I just wanted to say a huge THANK YOU to the TPB, Marti Amos, Owen Chambers and the entire Tpb Crew.

6 months ago when I started with TBP I had a great company. BUT; I had zero leads and the phone hadn't rung with a decent project for close to 2 years. I had hit rock bottom emotionally, mentally and was hating my job.

I had a great reputation, but zero systems and I had lost any market share of work within my region. I was wearing ALL the hats (my ex-business partner had just exited stage left) and was waaaay too busy to see the woods for the trees, let alone remember my kids names.

Fast forward 6 months........I'm now successfully turning my old 'company' into a seriously strong business.

People are talking, the phone is ringing, I'm sitting at a 100% lead conversion since mid November.....that's 6 out 6 projects secured, deposits paid, with a workload that now stretches' into ■■ and targeting a GP at 25% (unheard of before). I've had 22 enquiries from individuals wanting to work for me in the last 3 months (I haven't advertised any positions available). I have just had the best part of 5 weeks off, and the sites are humming...I've also planned my next holiday in April!! I visited the sites today........I don't really know why.......they don't need me any more!. I came back to my office; someone else is now doing all the old jobs that I previously hated, using systems that I'd never heard of.....I'm doing myself out of a job! I answer the phone.....another new pre-qualified lead from the new web-site.......they want to know how long they have to wait for us.......unheard of previously......my Admin manager (I never had one of those before) just laughs and tells me we're killing it, then hands me a back-costing report on the projects to date (who ever knew such information existed)!. Cashflow has been unbelievable and heading into ■■ we're looking forward to the strong return to profitability. Tomorrow morning I head in to my weekly management meeting where my foremen and construction manager will tell me where 'their' projects are at and will report to me, why they are ahead or behind programs......that they created, taken ownership and are implementing, using systems that are absolutely game changing.

With all this in mind, you should be able to now fill your schedule with the right activities that are going to get you to where you want to be. These tasks create what we call your Perfect Week—which should be recorded in your Default Diary. The Default Diary/Perfect Week is an excellent strategy that'll help you take control of your time and make you more money. It is one of the foundations of The Builder's Roadmap.

THE DEFAULT DIARY: YOUR PERFECT WEEK

To lead your team and your business, you must begin by leading yourself. To lead yourself, you must have a clear goal. Where are you heading? And who do you need to become in order to make your goals a reality?

For me, I needed to become more systemised and more structured. Now my Default Diary is my God. If it is important, it goes in my planner and that time slot is blocked out.

A Default Diary is an agenda/planner/appointment book where 20% of things that you do that give you the most value, enjoyment, productivity and results are scheduled to happen. No exceptions. To be a profitable builder, you must have your own Default Diary and use it to schedule your 20% of things that mean the most to you.

> *"I've been sticking to my default diary for 2 months now, and I no longer work on Sundays, but my output has been higher than before. Every time I wake up, I know which tasks I need to do; I don't have to try to remember where I left things off."*
>
> –Isaac C, Auckland

Your Default Diary will give you guidance and structure for your Perfect Week. It ensures that if it's in there, it's going to get done at that time. If it's not there in your Default Diary, it's very easy for you to override what's important, and then you're always feeling like, "I should be doing this, I should be doing that". This creates a constant state of overwhelm. Having a Default Diary is going to help get rid of that. You're going to prioritise what your ideal perfect week looks like and then structure everything else around that.

Start with your personal life. What is it that gives you great value and enjoyment? For me, it's helping my kids with their homework. At 5 pm, I help Ashton and Zak with their homework every night for 30 minutes. If it's in my planner, it gets done. It's also going to the gym, boxing, swimming, or cycling every day.

I also had a few personal things to tidy up. I had been a professional drinker since my college years. It had become a habit to have a glass or bottle of wine with a friend on the way home. This past October, I thought,

"Okay, I'm going to stop that (there's a great book about alcohol: This Naked Mind by Annie Grace)." I stopped drinking booze and it's been a game-changer. Clear headed, more productive, and better focus, plus fewer emotional ups and downs.

WHAT ARE YOU PUTTING IN YOUR MIND?

I've also been meditating and exercising every day, and I stopped reading the newspaper. I'd normally go to the cafe in the morning, read the newspaper and put all the negative stuff in my mind first thing. I then realised I could be listening to podcasts or whatever else that's going to help me cultivate a positive mindset and bring me closer to achieving my goals. One big question for you is: What are you putting in your mind? Are you engineering your brain for success?

Go and sit somewhere quiet, and get real with yourself. What am I doing (or not doing) that's not helping me? What's working well that I should do more of? Schedule in more of what's working and what you plan on working on in your Default Diary. Repeat this process every 90 days and review how you structure your week.

Your Default Diary/Perfect Week

	MONDAY 9	TUESDAY 10	WEDNESDAY 11	THURSDAY 12	FRIDAY 13
5AM					
6	Walk		Walk		
7	Work site checking		Work site checking	Work site checking	check on sub trades and orders for each job
8		Working on the business and TPB			Working on the business and TPB
9	Email replies and checking		Email replies and checking	Gym	
10	Update projects/Back costing/scheduling		Update projects/Back costing/scheduling	Appointments/potential clients	
		Gym			
11		Client catchup either by phone or meeting			Email replies and checking
12	check on sub trades and orders for each job		Miscellaneous works		Update projects/Back costing/scheduling
1PM	Quoting in office and booking new quotes		Quoting in office and booking new quotes	Client catchup either by phone or meeting	
2		Appointments/potential clients			Free time
3				Rugby Practice Kids	
4		Rugby Practice Kids			

For larger views of the tables featured in this book, scan the QR code at the end of each chapter to access a complete list of resources and images.

YOUR STOP DOING LIST

Your Stop Doing List is exponentially more important than your to-do list. Because your to-do list is only going to grow if you keep going the way you are. This is the official list inspired by the tasks you circled at the beginning of this chapter. Your Stop Doing List has the power to elevate how you run your business and your life. When you schedule and execute the big impact tasks daily, success is inevitable.

Take a look at one of our member's Stop Doing List and start thinking about what you would put on yours.

TPB THE PROFESSIONAL BUILDER — Stop Doing List

Task	Time Allocation	Action	Time Saving
Bookkeeping	2hrs	Outsource	2hrs
Paying Bills	2hrs	Delegate - Requires procedure	Eventually 2hrs
HR	2hrs	Outsource	2hrs
Phone Calls	2hrs	Outsource	2hrs
Legal	2hrs	Outsource	2hrs
Social Media/Advertising/Marketing	2hrs	Delegate Eventually	2hrs
Site Doc Prep	2hrs	Outsource	2hrs
Admin	2hrs	Outsource	2hrs
Procrastinating	4hrs	Eliminate	4hrs
Going to the Bowlo	6hrs	Reduce/Reschedule	2hrs
Picking up after the kids	8hrs	Retrain/Outsource	2hrs

TPB THE PROFESSIONAL BUILDER — Stop Doing List

Stop Doing Immediately	Plan to develop and then outsource or delegate in the next 90 days so I'm no longer doing it	Where I want to be what I should be doing
Managing a site being the foreman	Implement a system of on boarding a job then delegate to PM	Implement sales pipe line system
Pricing jobs that don't fit our business model	Implement a system of closing off a job then delegate to PM	Continue implementing introducer program to bring in good work
Unnecessary Site Visits	Refine invoicing/progress claims then delegate to accounts manager	Architect draftsman and real estate agent referrals
Over-commuting between sites	Implement a system of cost control and budget v actual and reporting then delegate to contracts admin	Business Development and Growth Plan
Materials ordering	Implement a system issuing of purchase orders build system then delegate to contracts admin	Working out the optimum size of current business
Stepping in to fill a void	Implement a system of tracking invoicing against purchase orders build system then delegate to contracts admin	Identifying next business
	Implement a dashboard reporting system then delegate input of data to key staff and then oversee weekly and monthly review	Staff development and Training Program
	Implement a process of approving a variation to a sub-contractor then delegate process to contracts admin and PM	Personal Development
	Implement a project by project monthly P&L then delegate data input to senior staff and oversee review	Oversee dashboard reporting system weekly and monthly
	Implement an overall business monthly P&L and delegate input to accounts manager and oversee review	Documenting processes then delegating management of the process
		Continual Upgrading Website & Marketing
		Simple monthly cash flow forecast model

When it comes to your business, there are likely plenty of tasks you're currently doing that aren't worth your time. You might be doing admin, going four months without a holiday, working with idiots and time wasters, not charging for the costs associated with contract variations, spending time going to get lunch for the guys, or working nights or on Sundays.

> *"The time management training I did with Marti and the couches was a game-changer. Now I'm in control of my calendar, and my time management issues dropped significantly."*

> —Brandon F, Auckland

Situations like this that don't serve you have got to become your non-negotiables. In other words, you will not do them anymore once they've made it to your Stop Doing list. The thought of this should feel like a massive relief. That's what owning a profitable building company is all about.

Change Your Thought Process

Now, I understand that all of what I'm asking you to do here seems easier said than done. I can hear all of your objections now. You might be thinking, "This is too hard," or, "That's great and all, but it isn't possible for me." You might even be getting anxious, thinking, "What if *this* happens? What if *that* happens?"

I work with a mindset coach. He's fantastic. He gave me a three-step process I want to share with you for dealing with negative thoughts and emotions. If you find yourself in a negative mindset or thinking negative thoughts, try this:

1. **Interrupt negative self-talk with awareness.** The most important thing is to be aware and stop the negative talk. You are not your thoughts. Pretend each thought is written on a piece of paper. Crumple up the paper into a little ball and throw it out the door.

2. **Have a clear, specific sense of what success looks and feels like.** Does success look like having your sales process working well? Is it when you have the foreman dialled in and doing the Toolbox Meeting agenda every Monday morning? When you're properly tracking labour hours? What does that look like, and how will you feel?

Find the next step that will move you forward toward your goal. Just one step. When you're in motion, it creates momentum that leads to more energy, and energy leads to results. What is the one step you can do right now that will bring you closer to where you need to be?

Also, rest assured we will go over exactly how you can stop doing the tasks that aren't helping and start doing what's most valuable for you to be doing in the next chapter. We'll really get to the core of what drives your motivation as we look at the bigger picture of your business and your role as the leader. You'll then learn how to delegate tasks to your team, at what rate to hire new team members, and in what order to claim your time in the chapter after that. All you need is the right information. With your Builder's Roadmap in hand, you've got this!

ACTION STEPS

1. Get clear on what success looks like for you and your business 12 months from now using The Vision Book.

2. Work out your Professional Builders Rate (PBR) with the PBR Calculator.

3. Map out your Stop Doing List to free up 8 hours (1 day per week) within the next 90 days.

Scan the code for all the resources:

MEMBER PROFILE: TRENT S.

A few years ago, Trent felt he was juggling too many balls in his business. He didn't have a clear structure for his team and back-end project processes. Trent's team struggled to keep track of their progress, and labour overruns were eating up his profits.

He was sick and tired of supervising his team all day and then catching up on unfinished paperwork in the evenings. All he wanted was to spend time with his family instead of locking himself away in his home office doing admin work at night. He could only dream of spending weekends snowboarding.

Trent hadn't had a day off in 3 years and was grinding through 10-hour days, seven days a week. Whenever he tried to step away from the business, all he could think about was how everything would fall apart without him holding it together.

Taking the Leap of Faith

He knew something needed to change quickly. Trent needed a clear structure and process for his business, so he took a leap of faith and joined TPB. First, we dialed in his goals for the next 12 months. Then, we assessed his current numbers, including company golden ratios, per-project profits, minimum margins, and his process for controlling work in progress in real-time. We focused on integrating team systems into his project management software, clarifying each team member's roles and KPIs (in their scorecard).

Everything was clearly laid out and documented from the foreman down to the apprentice. We also set up bonus schemes to ensure tasks were completed efficiently, on time, and to the necessary quality standards. After that, we ensured the team logged their hours in the project management software to reduce labour overruns, aiming to keep each project and stage within 5% of forecast labour hours.

Trent felt the weight slowly lifting off his shoulders; he no longer had to breathe down their necks to get them working. His phone stopped ringing constantly, and the team was getting their work done and reporting back daily through the project management software.

Within 12 months, Trent could take time off and enjoy a two-week snowboarding vacation in Colorado. His team kept things moving, hitting all the project milestones. All Trent had to do was a quick check-in with the team, leaving the rest of the day to enjoy his first real holiday in three years.

CHAPTER 2 – SUMMARY
LEAD YOUR BUSINESS SUCCESSFULLY

How you lead yourself is how you will lead your business.

People don't have business problems, they have personal problems that transcend over in to their business

- Get clear on your business and life mission. Clarity = power.

- Set yourself up for success with your environment and weekly/daily routine.

- Use the A-Z of operations to systemise the 'red lights' in your business with the Traffic Light approach.

- Buy back your time with the SAD principle:

  o Stop
  o Automate
  o Delegate

- Use both KPA (Key Performance Actions) and KPIs (Key Performance Indicators) with your teams on their scorecards to set them up for success.

- Map out exactly what your business looks like when it's finished with your BMD (Business Maturity Date).

LEAD YOUR BUSINESS SUCCESSFULLY

Leadership is the capacity to turn vision into reality.
–Warren G. Bennis

Over the next 90 days, we're going to reclaim 8 hours for you—a full working day. But you've got to do the work upfront to make that happen. To keep your motivation up, it's important to keep referring back to your *why* (what you wish to Have, Be, and Do). It can—and should—also go deeper than that. What's the bigger picture of your business that is going to *make* you implement these changes in your life? What makes you want to get out of bed in the morning and charge into action?

One of the biggest lessons I've learned is that how you lead yourself is how you will lead your business. The best way to make sure you're sticking to what's most important to you is to have a life mission statement that feeds your business mission statement.

Don't skip this step. This practice is crucial for you to clean up any mess you currently have and hold yourself accountable as a leader. It will ensure that you don't revert back to your old ways if things get a little tricky.

When people hear the word "mission statement," they think "business," but what about your *life* mission statement? How can you adhere to your business's mission if you're not clear on your own? The foundation of the Builder's Roadmap is to make your life as a business owner sustainable and to keep you loving your business, so integrating your personal values with those of your business is going to keep you in harmony with it as it grows. To become a better leader and ultimately create a business motivated by a bigger purpose, you need a life mission statement.

A good life mission statement covers two things:

1. Who you want to be
2. How you being *that person* will impact your life and the world

An example might be:

My life mission is to be present with the people around me because being generous with my time, energy, and expertise will keep me in a constant state of abundance and help others do the same.

As the owner of your own company, your life mission statement should be integrated into your company's mission statement. Your life mission is what you're in business for. If you can get more specific to include the people, places, and things you care about most, do it. Whatever works for you to keep you motivated.

Having a strong life mission statement will help keep you grounded, confident, and focused. Write it down neatly and on nice paper, put it on your office wall, and stick to it.

> *"One of the big things TPB taught me was having a big enough vision to fit my team's vision inside of it, and that's what we're doing. Our guys have been more willing to take more responsibility and level up their skills to execute their new tasks."*
>
> —Mark S, Fyshwick

WHAT'S THE MISSION OF YOUR BUSINESS?

At the Professional Builder, we define true profitability to be a journey. It's a journey that makes you a better person while creating a professional building company, that gives you both more money *and* more time. This is why it's crucial to lay out the values of your business and stick to them. An example business mission statement based on the life mission statement above might be:

Our business mission statement is to listen intently to our clients' desires because we take pride in how our craftsmanship can make their dreams come true.

Feel free to get creative with this and how it's worded; what matters most is that it shows your commitment to your clients' (and your) passion for what you do. If you need ideas, below are The Professional Builder's 4 core values.

TPB THE PROFESSIONAL BUILDER — **4 Core Values**

GROW OR DIE
You are either growing (Making Progress) or dying (Stagnating) there is no in between. Be quick to learn, ask questions, execute and improve in every area of life.

HEALTH & WEALTH
Set your PMD (Personal Maturity Date) with milestones along the way for fun, family, team, and personal pitstops. Prioritize your physical and mental fitness.

WORLD CLASS
Hold yourself to a higher standard of learning, implementing, measuring, and adjusting. Always ask how you can raise our collective standards and provide PSR (Problem, Solution(s), Recommendation)

MEMBER TRANSFORMATION
We can only win when our members win. Focus on consistent, life-changing moments and results for our community to create raving fans.

These are the values we hold close to our hearts and that guide our decision-making in different situations. Our team uses them as a guide to make accurate decisions. They're also used in our hiring process to see how we resonate with potential job applicants. We then use them every 90 days on our team's quarterly evaluations on a scale from 1 to 5 for how well each team member applies the company's values.

Being a business owner has the ability to raise the stakes high enough to force you to show up for yourself and choose better in order to get back to why you even started your business in the first place. Focusing on self-improvement and business development for the past 30+ years, I found mindfulness. It has helped me gain control of my mindset, and now I practise meditation daily. As I've become a better manager and a better leader, I've been able to run a better team—and expect more of them, pay them more, hold them accountable, shorten the feedback loop, and get better results in our business. This has, ultimately, allowed us to help more members achieve their goals.

I am a big believer in the adage, "People don't have business problems. They have personal problems that transfer over into their business." These problems might be a lack of discipline, a lack of focus, not being that motivated, not focusing on what *is* working in their business, refusing to hire people, not understanding their numbers, or avoiding marketing oneself in favour of waiting on referrals to come in. Each of these obstacles to a business owner's success is created by a self-limiting belief or deep-seated fear. Addressing this fear can be found in your daily programme.

I want you to take a moment to ask yourself, "What is it that energises me and gives me that burst of motivation?" Then, schedule two of those things into your Perfect Week/Default Diary:

1. One thing you could do for yourself in the morning to get your day started right

2. One thing you could do for yourself in the evening to decompress after a day of work

In the mornings, I meditate and exercise, which means going for a walk, going for a cycle, or going to the gym. And that repeats every day. Every Friday, my wife Kelly and I go out for a weekly 'date lunch.' Then I structure in a bit of quality time with myself at night: some guilty pleasures like some F1 Drive to Survive, The Sopranos reruns, or playing the guitar.

Once I have my most important meetings with my most important clients (myself and my family) out of the way, I feel ready to take on the high-value 20% of business activities that I've determined make the biggest difference with the methods we discussed in Chapter 1. This flow has made me (and those I have coached) a lot more productive and a lot more profitable.

Add one more thing to your morning and night routine every 90 days until you hit that sweet spot that works for you. As a business owner, having both mental peace and emotional stability must come first. Not having one of these things can wreak havoc on the system. You must protect your mojo.

One huge contributing factor to your mental peace and emotional stability—and thus your productivity—is your work environment. Set yourself up for success from the start by making sure you have no distractions and feel at ease to really focus in the place where you do your work daily. Ask yourself:

Is my environment at home, work, or the cafe the best place to get things done?

REFINE YOUR WORK ENVIRONMENT

I work away from the office on Monday, Wednesday, and Friday. I love going to my favourite cafe in St Heliers by the beach where we live. On Tuesdays and Thursdays, we all work in the office in the city on the waterfront.

I put on my headphones and take my notebook and iPhone. Honestly, I get more done working out of the office than I do in the office. In the office, there are team conversations, chats, and emails, which distracts my productivity.

Figure out what the best environment is for you. It might be somewhere away from home or away from the office that will allow you to hone in on only the most strategic elements of running your business—the 20% that's creating 80% of your results as you move your business forward. Lead yourself and thus your business.

BUILDER'S ROADMAP TIP:

DON'T LET PEOPLE WHO SUCK YOUR TIME AND ENERGY GET IN THE WAY OF YOUR WORK!

You are the sum of the five people you are around the most—and also the environment you place yourself in. Think of the people and places you interact with often. Do they zap you or sap you? Your energy is a precious resource. Treat it with respect.

I encourage you to do a friend audit. Upon going through your friends list, ask yourself: *Do they zap (energise) or sap (drain) me?*

SET YOUR DAYS UP FOR SUCCESS

At The Professional Builder, we advise our members to structure their days around what's going to make them the most productive. The following guidelines will make your Perfect Week/Default Diary the most effective and stress-free it can be:

1. Work that is going to have the biggest impact and requires the most brain power should be done first thing in the morning when you are fresh (after your coffee, of course).

2. Schedule work tasks in batches of time. It's very difficult for your brain to swap from quoting to going on site to doing sales. So, block each type of work off into 90-minute to 2-hour boxes.

3. The goal is not to fill your week up with anything and everything. The goal is to have about 70% of this structured and 30% free for stuff that just happens—'cause shit's going to happen.' Stuff's

going to come up, whether it's concrete not arriving on time or carpenters calling in sick, so you're going to need some gaps in your Default Diary to be able to respond to it.

4. Work towards scheduling a completely free day when you're not thinking about the business—when you're not working on the business at all. Perhaps this day is every Friday. This is going to be a massive game-changer for you if you're not already doing this. The mind needs space and clarity to be productive. Scheduling rest and recreation into your perfect week/ Default Diary—and sticking to it—is going to make you more productive in all aspects of your life.

For example, one of our members, Russell Clark, takes every Friday off to:

- Go fishing
- Work on his Mustangs
- Or work on his holiday beach house back in Onemana, New Zealand

Another member, Hayden Simpson, would take Wednesdays off to renovate his own house and now takes days off during the week for his son's budding motocross career.

YOUR A-Z OF OPERATIONS

Now, let's get into the "what" of running your business What we're discussing next is the meat and potatoes of your workday. As a business owner, you need a clear view of your whole business to know what your next step is (and then where to go from there). Here are the A-Z of operations for your construction business—all the working parts:

TPB THE PROFESSIONAL BUILDER

A-Z of Operations

START HERE

Marketing
- TPB Marketing Pillars To Do The Heavy Lifting For Sales
- TPB Facebook Quick Grab Ads™
- TPB 1% Referral System™
- Website Domination™
- Lead Magnet Builder:
- Attract Your Ideal Target Market

Sales
- Qualifying Questionnaire
- Triage Call Phone Script
- Site Visit Agenda
- Info Pack™
- Preliminary Budget
- High Converting Quote
- Quote As An Action Plan™
- Keep Warm Auto-Responder Sequence

Pricing
- Target Margin 20%
- Forecast VS Actual Per Stage (5%)
- Overhead Recovery Margin
- Project Management Fee
- 20-Point Pricing For Profit Checklist™

Contract Signed
- 18-Point Contract Checklist™
- Deposit
- Payment Schedule
- Enter Job Management

Schedule
- Sub-Trades
- Labour By Stage
- Progress Milestones
- Materials
- Selections

Project Set-Up
- Order materials
- Phone contact RE start date
- Pre-Construction Meeting With Foreman & Team
- Scope Of Works & Budget Break Down With Foreman

Lead Not Converted

Send Thank You Email

Add To Newsletter, Email Sequence OR Re-Targeting Campaign

Handover
- Gift to client
- Interview for testimonial

Complete Project

Variations
- Signed Off
- Invoiced Weekly
- Admin Fee Charged
- VO Form

Project Margin on Project
- 60-Point Profit Protection Checklist™
- 151 Ways To Make An Extra $500k 1k On A Job™
- TPB Profitable Projects

Complete Stage
- 287-Point Quality Assurance Checklist™

Unpaid Project
- Follow Debtor Management & Collections Process

Weekly Systems
- Invoice & Pay Team
- PO System
- Track Labour Forecast VS Actual

Update Client
- TPB Client Communication

Start Project

Team Improvement
- Scorecards
- Team Vi-sion
- Rules Of The Game™
- Bonus & Incentives™
- Quarterly Performance Review
- Weekly Construction Meetings
- Scorecard
- Daily Stand Ups

Hiring
- Job Description
- How To Hire & Onboard High Quality Carpenters™
- Interview Process
- Reference Checks
- Employment Contract

Induct
- Onboarding Framework
- Onramp Workbook
- Align With Company Values
- Daily Stand Ups

Back Costing
- Work In Progress In Real Time
- Labour Forecast Vs Actual (+5%)
- Materials & Sub-Contractors

Select 1 Strategy From TPB Roadmap

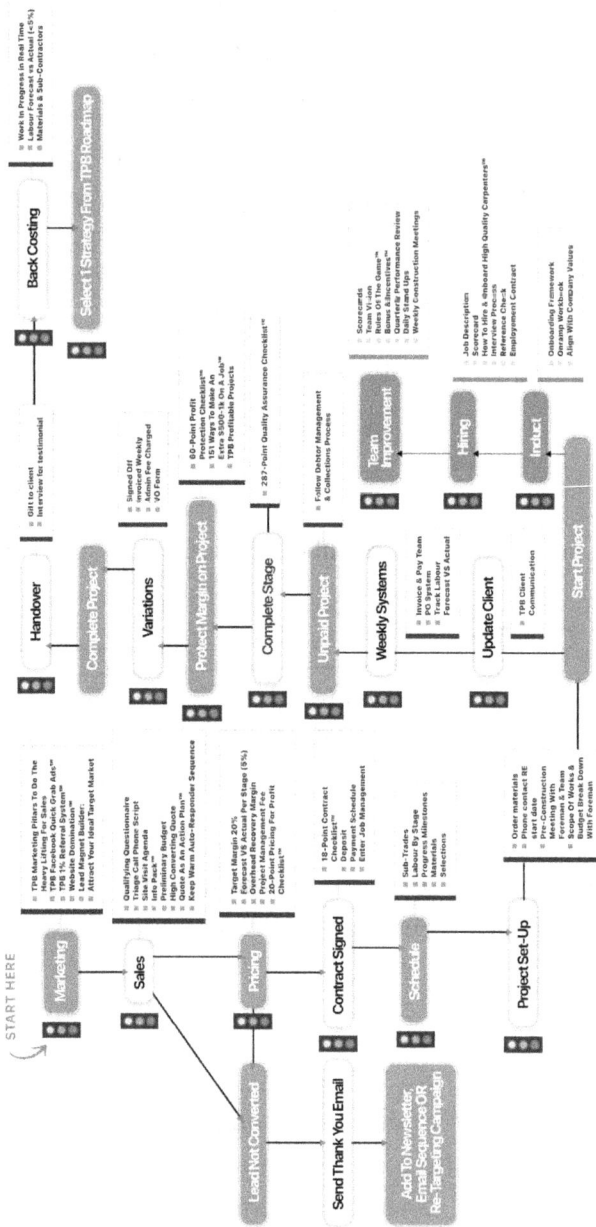

For larger views of the tables featured in this book, scan the QR code at the end of each chapter to access a complete list of resources and images.

You can use this A-Z of Operations flow chart or create one of your own that suits your business.[1]

---

[1] You can download it from the Resources page on our website. Having this around will give the members of your team a clear visual of their role in the business.

> *"A year ago, we were swamped with work and juggling too many things. Marti helped us set a clear direction. Now, we have the clarity we need and are even more laser-focused on how to reach our goals. It gives us a lot of confidence."*
>
> — Nicky G & Corey G, Wellington

To know what areas need the most attention now, assign a traffic light colour to each operation:

RED LIGHT TASKS

Deem something "red light" if it's an area of pain or frustration—or it just isn't working well. These are the big holes in your bucket, like too much time spent doing the low-dollar-value tasks we discussed in Chapter 1 (for example: going to the merchant or doing payroll or invoicing). For items like this that end up on your Stop Doing list, The Builder's Roadmap has a way to get them off your desk and handled for good.

IMPLEMENTING YOUR STOP DOING LIST WITH THE "MY LAST DAY" METHOD

One way to hold yourself accountable to truly stopping an activity you do regularly is to apply the Business Maturity Date (BMD) principle to the roles you're currently doing. This way, you have time to secure who is going to replace you in getting things done or what systems you will have in place to improve that particular item. Write the task down along with the last day you will do it:

"My last day on the tools will be…"

"My last day pricing will be…"

"My last day taking a project with less than 20% gross profit will be…"

"My last day tolerating labour hours being slower than 5% versus forecast will be…"

The Stop Doing List is intended to give you clarity and confidence on what you should be focusing on in order to bring more enjoyment and profit into your business. To go along with the example of the life mission statement and the business mission statements used above, the motivation to stop doing so many tasks is directly correlated with being more present with people, whether that be family members, clients, or team members. Your mission statements should always be at the core of everything you do and drive you to do higher-value tasks within the business, no matter how tempting it may get to go back to the way things were.

When letting go of certain responsibilities you've always had, it's okay to get SAD. In fact, it's great! It's preferred. It's recommended.

What am I talking about? Well, part of the Builder's Roadmap is to integrate what we call the SAD Principle. Of the tasks you're going to stop doing yourself, look at each one and decide if you should:

1. **S**top it altogether
2. **A**utomate it
3. **D**elegate it

Here's exactly what I mean:

THE SAD PRINCIPLE

Get out that list you initially made in Chapter 1. Mark each one as either Stop, Automate, or Delegate according to the following criteria:

STOP

Not every task needs to get done—full stop. Cross out things you think might actually be a waste of time for *anyone* to be doing. Ask yourself, "Is this task being completed bringing me closer to my goals? Or...could it be impeding them?"

For example:

- Reading the newspaper

- Accepting jobs below 20% gross profit

- Dealing with time wasters whose scope doesn't match their budget and who have unrealistic expectations

- Pricing projects for free and wasting 20-100 hours of work for no pay

AUTOMATE

As for the tasks that still need to get done somehow, let's think outside the box for a minute. In this day and age, it doesn't necessarily need to be a human. The best way to get the benefits of a task being done without hiring someone is to get technology to take care of it.

For example:

- Payroll

- Project management (use software like Buildertrend)

- Sales process automation

- Email sequences

- AI for some marketing tasks

DELEGATE

To determine if a task can/should be delegated, start asking yourself some questions:

- Do I need a part-time office manager?

- Could someone else do site setup?

- Should I outsource my pricing?

- Do I have enough workflow to bring on board a full-time estimator?

- Who else could do my payroll? Could it be someone on, say, $35 an hour?
- Could the hammer hand, labourer, or one of my carpenters go to the merchant for me?

After realising that you have to delegate some of the tasks taking up most of the time you'd rather/should be spending doing something else, you may find you'll have to hire your first or second person in the office, whether that's your loving wife or someone else who can help you, like a bookkeeper, part-time marketing coordinator or a student.[2] What matters most is how you approach this. The profitable builder knows exactly what they want done, how they want it done, and how to communicate it well.

When it comes to outsourcing tasks for your business, memorise this phrase:

Delegate, don't abdicate.

Abdicating is saying, "Yeah, dude. You're the foreman. Have at it." This ends up causing you to get frustrated when the person you assigned to the job doesn't do it the right way, and everything falls behind. Delegating, on the other hand, is giving your team a system and a process to follow, covering everything from site setup and checklists to how they submit their timesheets, plan the job, and order materials on the first day of the month. Delegating stems from a system that repeats and is done the same way each and every time. It's like a bowling alley lane that gives guardrails for your team to allow them to run faster.

When the process runs smoothly, everybody wins. Steps are clear enough for team members to follow, setting them up for success, and you, the building business owner, to make more by working less. One of our

---

[2] Auckland University of Technology has a Co-op Programme. Students have to go and work for 40 hours a week for 10 weeks for free at the end of their final year to complete their degree. We used to pay our students $100 a week. You may be able to get a student on a co-op or an intern programme to help you or you could hire a virtual assistant.

members, Brent T from Sydney, got off the tools and focused solely on his business and building systems. He went from making $66,000 net profit to $392,000 net profit in 12 months. That's a $326,000 pay raise by plugging the holes in his business without working more hours.

"We were just surviving, very low margins or I was dropping my margins to win the job, poor cash flow, not knowing our backend costs, I was getting very stressed, lack of communication between site and office, with a limited project management system.

First up I needed to get my team back and focused with a clear direction so I issued job descriptions /scorecards, rules of the game and doing weekly meetings. - The Results -This has made a huge difference, everyone has a clear understanding of their roles, great communication, the team is focused/driven, we have a better-balanced company.

Having a very clear picture of how the projects are tracking, time/ materials against the cost. Communication between office and site is on point, the system is perfect for our needs. Also, We have created "The Labour Tracker". This is an excel spreadsheet the foreman uses on the site using an Ipads to track their time against every individual carpentry task cost as well, this work really well for a day to day tool.

I rebuilt all my quoting recipes to suit our projects and needs. I also started to trust in myself and the product we deliver and less worried about what the other builders that I was tendering against were doing. - The Result - Higher margins sitting between 20-25% GP.

I meet every week with my bookkeeper/admin team we look at my company figures, WIP, company overheads, we keep all variations and invoices up to date, this keeps a healthy cash flow coming into the business."

-Brent T, Sydney

IF HIRING SOMEONE WON'T SOLVE IT, MAKE USE OF SERVICES FOR YOUR BUSINESS

I spent 15 minutes walking down the street in Newmarket to get the mail from the Post office box every day for two years. It was great walking past all the retail shops. It was also 15 minutes walking back, so I realised this task was taking me half an hour each day, five days a week. That's two and a half hours! That's 125 hours per year. When I realised this, I was like, "Holy crap! And I'm the guy complaining that I don't have enough time to go to the gym." So, I started looking at my options.

I could have **S**topped this task altogether, but then there would be a lot of important stuff that we wouldn't get. Bills would pile up, for example, so that wasn't an option.

I could have **A**utomated it, but a way to do that doesn't exist for physical letters.

I could have **D**elegated it to my assistant Isabella, but then that would have taken time away from *her* job.

This one task wasn't enough to justify actually hiring someone to be a part of my team, so I delegated it to Isabella to find a solution.

Isabella ended up calling the courier company, and their options worked well. If I had hired Isabella and it took her two hours and I was paying her $60,000 a year/$1,200 a week/$30 an hour, it would cost me $60 dollars a week/$240 a month/$3,000 a year of her time going to get the mail. Calling the courier company, on the other hand, meant they'd go get our mail and deliver it twice a week for just $75 a month.

I share this with you to show you that there are always solutions to what you need to stop doing yourself. You just have to think outside of the box sometimes.

> *"We never had a problem working 12-13 hours a day because [we] thought that was the norm. But after joining TPB, we understood we didn't have to do it, so we shifted from working more to working smart, always looking three to four steps ahead."*
>
> —Joel P & Michaela P, Brisbane

DEEM TASKS WHERE YOU NEED TO CHANGE YOUR APPROACH FAST AS "RED LIGHT!"

Something you deem "red light" can also be something that can't be stopped, automated, or delegated. It's something integral to the business that needs immediate attention but merely requires you to stop the *way* you're doing it. This is where systems come in. I like to think of systems as follows:

Saving

You

Stress

Time

Energy

Money

> *"After joining TPB, the biggest change for me is the amount of time I'm making up now. I'm able to get behind the curtain and compress time in a way that I haven't been able to do before, where I feel like I can make up for lost time and recover that."*
>
> —Michael M, Nelson

Systems run your company. You hire and train the right people to run those systems and then hold them accountable. Hold weekly meetings with your team to discuss two things:

1. **Key Performance Actions (KPAs):** The tasks assigned to a team member that propel a project forward are called Key Performance Actions (KPAs). There might be two or three key tasks that each person in each role does each and every week that is critical for that role. And we're going to make sure that we are inspecting those on a regular basis. To keep track of what each person in the team is doing, we use Slack[3] and Asana[4].

2. **Key Performance Indicators (KPIs):** There is going to be a number or a metric that is tied to each of these tasks. For the foreman, it might be billable hours broken down by stage and milestone. The goal is to get actual labour hours by stage to within 5% of forecast. For an office administrator, it might be the number of debtor days or percentage of debtors. When you have a key number for each task, it makes life much easier and more focused. These numbers are Key Performance Indicators (KPIs).

INSPECT WHAT YOU EXPECT

If you don't monitor what your team is doing, they won't be aware that you're monitoring them and that they need to be following the system. You need to take your business seriously. You can't rely on great people. You need to build great systems. And most people have life problems that transfer over into business. So, make sure that you are inspecting what you expect, whether you use:

- A sprint board like we do
- A scrum board with Post-it notes of different colours

---

[3] Slackbot is an automated bot that messages us around 8 AM every day, asking, "What did you work on yesterday? What are you working on today? Is there anything stopping your progress?" This allows us to plan for the day and show each other what we're doing. It's also a good reminder to ensure the continuity and completion of our tasks. Visibility makes the team accountable because it's like, "Did you do it? Yes or no?"

[4] Asana is for task management, which works really well for delegating projects. It's like an online to-do list, and it provides a lot of clarity around what everyone's doing and allows you to cross tasks off of a list in real time since communication with team members is frequent.

- Asana
- Trello
- Basecamp

…or any other software for managing your projects like Buildertrend.

Also, make sure that you're clear on your on-site trade times. Project management software[5] is a great tool for this. If you make a change to the timeline, it automatically sends a notification to the team members affected by that specific change. This software is a great way to manage any variations, structure your week, and communicate with your subcontractors and clients.

Red light tasks are your big priorities that you need to do right away and one of the tools that you can use is The 2 Week Sprint. You want to break down your priority tasks into clear tasks you can do over the next two weeks. Take hiring an Office Manager as an example. This could be broken down into two-week sprints like defining the role scope, advertising, hiring, onboarding, and finally training. Each of these two-week sprints can be broken down further. Hiring could be split into sub-tasks like screening, phone interview, site interview, personality test, trial tasks, reference check, offer of employment, and contract signing.

ORANGE LIGHT TASKS

These are things that are pressing but not as pressing as the red light stuff. For example, you might need to turn the sales and marketing taps on full blast to accelerate your business. Mark it "red" for the *next* round of 90-day projects.

GREEN LIGHT TASKS

What's green is what's working fine for now. Carry on as you normally would. There is always something that *is* working. Thank heavens.

---

[5] Some examples include Buildertrend, Buildxact and Rave.

Now that you have some insight on how to start on the right foot to help your business run smoothly let's find what the next logical steps to take should be based on the rate at which your business will mature. This is determined by the date at which you are able to measure if you've reached your goals for your business. I now want to walk you through a critical concept for you to be familiar with as a leader called your Business Maturity Date (BMD).

YOUR BUSINESS MATURITY DATE (BMD)

Think about what you want your business to look like in 18 to 24 months. Perhaps you're working in the area you enjoy the most, your zone of genius, and your business is making the kind of money you want in order to have the life you want. Your BMD is the exact date by which you predict this will all be in place.

There are three things you need to do to make this Business Maturity Date a reality:

1. **Make a decision:** What are you actually building? What does your future look like?

2. **Pick a date:** When will you build this out by? When will the company be finished? I would suggest 18 to 24 months to give you enough time, but it's also short enough to still motivate and excite you. If you must make this date further in the future, I would suggest 36 months (3 years) as the maximum.

3. **Make it public:** Let your team know how they're involved in the changes you're making and allow them the opportunity for growth. There will be plenty of opportunities for them to step up as the company approaches its Business Maturity Date. Roles to fill will naturally arise as you systemise, decide who you're hiring next, deliberate what each job description should include, communicate

how each team member can "win" (what's in it for them?), and measure how the business wins.

So, 18 to 24 months from now, what does your business look like in terms of profit, revenue, number of jobs you're doing, gross margin, days off per week, and vacations you take per year?

Also, who do you need to hire next to make your desired BMD a reality—in order to get off the hamster wheel of doing everything yourself? Our BMD sheet and diagram (shown below) will help you keep track and decide who needs to be hired next in the team positions in your construction business.

	Your Existing	Your Projected	Your BMD
Enter Your Desired Net Profit:	$ 150,000	$ 500,000	$ 1,000,000
Enter Your Fixed Costs (Incl. Your Salary):	$ 150,000	$ 380,000	$ 800,000
Total Gross Profit:	$300,000	$880,000	$1,800,000
Enter Your Target Gross Margin	17%	24%	25%
Your Required Annual Sales **(Gross Profit+Gross Margin)**	$ 1,764,706	$ 3,666,667	$ 7,200,000
Enter Your Average Sale Value **(total sales + no. of jobs done)**	$ 80,000	$ 450,000	$ 950,000
Number of Projects You Need to Complete each Year	22.06	8.1	7.6
Enter Your Conversion Rate **(no. of jobs won + no. of quotes done)**	80%	50%	66%
Number of jobs You Require to quote Year:	27.6	16.3	11.5
If working for 10 months **Number of Leads You Require Each Month:**	2.8	1.6	1.1

Business Maturity Date

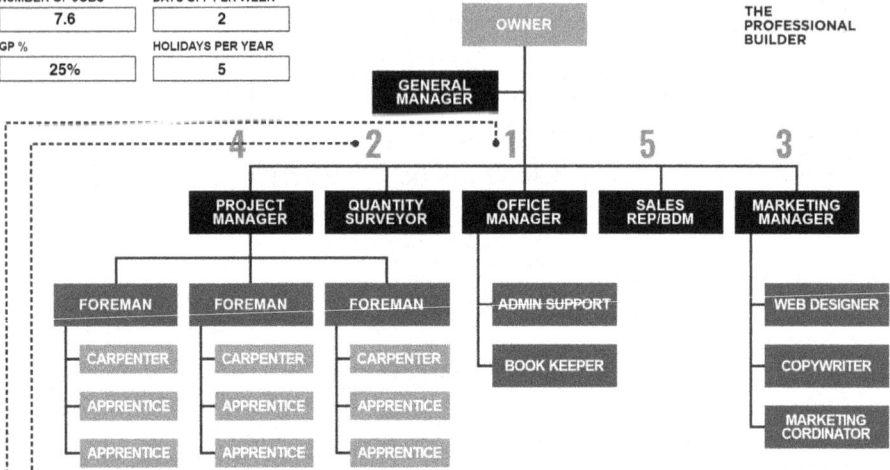

EXAMPLE		YOURS	
#1 BMD for	OFFICE ADMIN	#1 BMD for	
#2 BMD for	QS-ESTIMATING	#2 BMD for	
#3 BMD for	MARKETING	#3 BMD for	
#4 BMD for	PROJECT MANAGEMENT	#4 BMD for	
#5 BMD for	SALES	#5 BMD for	

This timeline of 18 to 24 months dictates at what rate the tasks from your Freedom Finder will be effective. It will allow you to set up KPIs to make sure you're on track. These should be discussed at weekly meetings as they are the metric tied to measuring whether each task has been completed successfully.

For example:

- When will you hire your office manager?
- When will you hire an in-house estimator?

- When will you promote one of your foremen to project manager?

You then line this up with your cashflow forecast to ensure you have a clear list of tasks for that role (from your Stop Doing List) and at least three to six months of salary set aside for them.

Do you know how many hours this will save you? A project manager can free up 20-25 hours per week. The next important thing is how you use the time you've bought back. You may want to set aside 10 hours to reclaim your weekends and one night per week. The other 10 hours might be for working ON the business to install better systems for onsite, sales and marketing, back costing projects, and team training.

> *"The mindset training with Marti is a game changer. Now, I view business as a tool to get where I want in life. The business is here to serve us, not for us to serve the business. So, our focus is to have a business that you run rather than the business running you."*
>
> –Joel P & Michaela P, Brisbane

In the next chapter, we'll go deeper into how to perfect your meetings. A lot of it involves communication and accountability through visibility. This is where your skills at managing people come in. We're going to discuss how to interact, motivate, and incentivise your team so that you focus on what you need to do and leave the rest of the business's operations in the hands of those individuals who you chose, as part of your team.

ACTION STEPS

1. Get clear on your business's 4 Core Values. Then have a session with your team on how everyone will apply and LIVE these values.

2. Implement the "My last day (pricing, set up sites, etc) will be…" strategy.

3. Map out your Business Maturity Date (BMD) and build the business you know is possible.

Scan the code for all the resources:

MEMBER PROFILE: BEN T.

Ben runs a $10 million construction company in New Zealand, working just four days a week. This is achievable due to his implementation of systems and a culture of accountability that allows his team to manage the business independently.

Ben's team includes two office managers handling accounts and pricing, and eight site workers. His role is to lead and empower his team through proven management processes. He utilises frameworks like the PSR (Problem, Solutions, Recommendation) formula and the RICE (Revenue, Impact, Certainty, Ease) framework to develop his team into problem solvers who can take charge without needing constant supervision.

THE ART OF DELEGATION

A significant part of Ben's success lies in his delegation strategy. By setting up an incentive scheme for his foremen, he ensures that project milestones are met on time and within budget. This setup has allowed him to step back from the daily grind, confident that his team can handle the operational aspects of the business.

Ben's approach to running his business involves setting up efficient systems. He trained his team to handle tasks smoothly, so the business runs well even when he's not there. This has given him the freedom to work on other projects, spend more time with his family, and train for Ironman competitions and mountain biking.

He's been able to take extended vacations without worrying about his business, including spending five weeks in the UK with his wife Gemma and their three children. During this time, his team not only managed ongoing projects but also secured new ones.

Ben has also made sure his company's name is visible throughout New Zealand, from signs on every project to logos on all company tools and vehicles. This consistent branding has significantly boosted his company's visibility and reputation.

BUILD A GREAT TEAM

Cultivating a strong sense of community within his team is crucial to Ben. He and his wife treat their employees like family, offering support and guidance beyond work-related matters. This approach has fostered a loyal and motivated team, many of whom have been with the company for over five years.

Strategic decision-making is another cornerstone of Ben's success. He transitioned from using standard house plans to employing an in-house draughtsperson, allowing for more customisation and client satisfaction. This shift has streamlined the design process and strengthened client relationships.

Financial visibility is critical to Ben's business strategy. Using Xero and Buildertrend for accounting and project management, he tracks expenses and cash flow in real-time. This system allows him to forecast and manage finances, reducing stress and ensuring the company's financial health.

Ben's story illustrates the power of effective leadership, strategic planning, and robust systems. By empowering his team and fostering a culture of accountability, he has created a construction business that allows him to enjoy a balanced and fulfilling life. His journey offers valuable lessons for other construction business owners looking to achieve similar success.

CHAPTER 3 – SUMMARY
BUILD A WINNING TEAM

Alone we can go fast, together we can go further.

Build your team and they build the business, rather than feeling stuck on the Builder's Hamster Wheel or like you have built yourself a prison

- Build the company values from what personal values are important to you.

- Get scorecards for each role so the team knows whether they are winning (or not).

- Hire to buy back your time, rather than to just increase capacity.

- When and how to prepare for your new team members to hit the ground running.

- The meetings and systems your team need to succeed.

- How to run toolbox and construction meetings effectively.

- PSR - The greatest simple management tool to teach your team:

  o Problem
  o Solution(s)
  o Recommendation

BUILD A WINNING TEAM

Team-building is so important that it is virtually impossible for you to reach the heights of your capabilities or make the money that you want without becoming very good at it.
—Brian Tracy

As you go along relinquishing your responsibility in certain areas of your business, you may or may not have some resistance to it. There's an easy way to tell: do any of the following thoughts sound familiar?

I can do it all myself.

Clients only want to deal with me.

I need to be on site; otherwise, everything turns to custard!

If this is you, please understand that dropping these limiting beliefs will bring you closer to your goal of getting back 8 hours (1 day of your work week[1]) within the next 90 days. Building a more profitable building business takes a highly skilled team, and you're the one who's going to lead them—not do their job for them (even if they ask you for help). In this

---

[1] Take half that time to clear your head and restore your sanity (spend time with family, exercise, do your hobbies). The other 4 hours should be used to work on the business, but only doing the high skill, high fun tasks from your Fun/Skills Matrix like installing systems or ensuring productivity on site—the $1000-an-hour tasks that are going to greatly improve your business and your quality of life.

chapter, you'll gain the right mindset to lead your team to success with proven systems that have worked for the building business owners we have coached to success. Even if you haven't hired your first person in the office yet, the following should be how you start any hiring process and proceed with your current team to get everyone working towards the same goal.

> *"50% of my staff has been with me for over five years and I can keep them thanks to the mindset shift from builder to business owner Marti talks about. I've always given them incentives to keep moving forward within my company."*

—Ben T, Twizel

FIRST AND FOREMOST, LEAD WITH YOUR PERSONAL VALUES

Combine your personal values with your company values and vision.

- When being a client yourself, you might wish to have friendly experiences, so a personal value tied to this might be, "I want clients to have a great customer experience."

- When being a client yourself, you value your time and standards, so a personal value tied to this might be, "I want the client's requests to be carried out with speed and accuracy."

- When being a client yourself, you want what you paid for, so a personal value tied to this might be, "I want to make the client's dream build a reality."

HOLD A VALUES MEETING ASAP

Create a meeting (soon) in which all members get together and share their personal values. Don't worry—this should only take about 30-45 minutes. Have everyone come up with their top three values and display them on a screen or white board. Then, come up with three or four company values as a group that reflect the fusion of everyone's values.

Your team needs to buy into the vision of what's important to your business. If they participate in the planning of its vision, they will go to work completely motivated to work for a company that has a piece of them in it.

The format of your company values depends on how each team member's values can be combined, but we suggest having one overarching value with a definition that has three sub-values. This way, it's easy to remember and tie the three together. For example:

Company value: Every build we do and every client interaction is world-class. **What this means:** World-class means on time, under budget, and with the same care we would have for our own dream build.

NOW WHAT?

Once you have your company's value clearly stated and defined, embed its essence into your daily culture. Put them up on your office walls and add them into your company manuals. Use them for hiring and display them on your website. Include them in your work process and ask people how your values resonate with them. Definitely include it in your marketing. In short, put it up everywhere so people can see what you stand for.

It's important to have this be visible so you, your clients, and your team members know what to expect from the work put out by your company. These standards you've set should be non-negotiable. You might even have to get rid of people based on these values. The point of having this in place is so that when you're away or on vacation, you know that you can trust your team to make the right decisions.

> *"I just returned from a two-week vacation in Europe and didn't check my email even once. The systems I implemented from TPB made this possible. I returned and found the business running smoothly, with zero hiccups."*
>
> –Adam C, Florida

CHOOSE ONLY TO WORK WITH PEOPLE WHO ALIGN WITH YOUR VALUES

To decide if any changes need to be made to your current team, let's take a moment and do an exercise. Get out a sheet of paper to write your answers to the following questions:

1. If I fired all the people on my team now, who would I rehire?

2. Who do I need to move on?

3. Are we overstaffed in one particular area at the moment?

4. Who's my number 1?

5. Who's my number 10?

It's okay if you simply don't need someone or are not benefiting from having them on your team.[2] They just might not be a good fit. Maybe you've got five foremen, and only three are producing. You might be top-heavy in one area of your business and lacking personnel in another. You've got to be making these hard decisions as a boss or your business will not grow. Of course, respect and observe HR and legal considerations when letting go of personnel, but don't be afraid to do what's best for the company. Your life mission, business mission, and a life of financial freedom are the goals

---

[2] One of our members recently went from 18 to 13 carpenters and increased productivity, accountability, and profitability! Think of your business as a sports team rather than a family. A sports team needs everyone to know their role and bring their A-game to work every day.

here. If you have to let someone go, they are free to pursue other better-suited opportunities for themselves.

> *We have 18 full-time employees, and having TPB's team management systems has helped us keep them accountable. We're clear on the goals they need to hit and ensure everything is in order.*
>
> —John C, Texas

Tough conversations need to happen when accountability is low.

Accountability comes from:

- Scorecards for each role
- Expectations of the role and responsibilities
- Measurement of success ("Are you winning?" Usually a metric like timeline for a foreman, invoices sent and collected for an Office Manager, Labour hours within 5% for a Project Manager).
- Feedback by leaders, both formally and informally, via coaching and course correction.

So, before you start having tough conversations, address accountability by making sure there are clear expectations, a way of measuring success, and that feedback is given as frequently as possible.

If these three conditions do not exist, tough conversations usually turn into crippling conversations. Chats that require a huge amount of conviction and planning because you need to coach, handle objections, and course correct someone who is way off course.

This is avoidable by being clear on expectations, measurement, and feedback with job scorecards and regular check-ins.

THE VALUES OF EACH ROLE TO BE DECIDED BY YOU

When looking at your A-Z of operations, assign personal values you want each person in each role to uphold, even if you haven't hired someone in that role yet. For example, for your QS/Estimator it will be attention to detail and constant improvement to the pricing, project management, and back-costing processes to get within 5% of the total labour hours forecast for each project, broken down by stage.

List each role on a sheet of paper, and under each one, list the values they should uphold. You'll refer to them later when creating your job ads for new hires and for training.

YOUR VALUES AS METRICS FOR EXISTING TEAM MEMBERS

For your systems for each role to be measurable, they need metrics that will let you know they are working. Create your metrics in accordance with your values.

After you've created your KPIs, add specific KPAs that align with your clearly defined values for each role. Go through your list for each role in your company and ask yourself two questions:

1. How well is this person living the company's values?

2. How well are they performing compared to their scorecard?

Write down your reflections on each team member's performance every 90 days. Each member can have a sheet like the one below whereby you can measure their KPIs and KPAs.

MISSION FOR FOREMAN:

To be the main driving force of the project and manage the team

1. Having the projects completed to timeline

2. Have the materials used with minimal wastage

3. To complete stages to our quality standards

4. To manage the team's day-to-day output and focus

5. To communicate closely with Brent

OUTCOMES // KPIS // KPAS:

- **Update the project schedule and report it to Brent in our weekly catchup**
  - o Schedule is updated Weekly using _____ to show the actual Vs the forecast.

- **Coordinate with sub trades to**
  - o Use _____ to coordinate subtrades

- **Complete project to within X% of completion date**
  - o Project must be completed to within X% of the completion date

- **Order materials on the Thursday for the following week**
  - o For every additional delivery weekly $X into the social fund from the whole team on the project.

- **Actual material costs to be within X% of forecast**
  - o During our back-costing exercise have each stage of project to be within X% of materials

- **Pass Quality Checklist first time**
  - o Pass the quality checklist for each stage first time around by 90% +

- **Run weekly toolbox meeting**
  - o Update the site during the week using the toolbox meeting agenda
  - o Run any updates back via Brent

- **Run daily stand-up with team**
  - o Run quick daily 5-minute standup at 4:45 each day to cover actions from day and to-dos for tomorrow.
  - o Send voice clip or call to Brent by 5:30 with day's update.
- **Weekly 1-1 session with Brent each Friday afternoon**
  - o Use the scorecard in the session

GET YOUR TEAM MEMBERS TO CARE

Now, how do you get people to *care* about the values you've envisioned for their role? Two words: career progression. To get a member of your team to buy into your vision, show a clear way for them to progress up through your company, and they will work hard to climb the ladder.

BUILDER'S ROADMAP TIP:

MAKE SURE YOUR TEAM WANTS TO WORK FOR YOUR COMPANY.

If your team members want to leave, it means you don't have a strong company culture. If you've got a great company culture, everyone's getting paid well, and they have a clear career path and progression, there's no reason for someone to leave. You need to have a big enough vision for your company and for your team members' vision to fit inside and allow them to achieve their goals.[3]

Dead-end jobs have high turnover rates because people simply don't see themselves living with that job long-term, thus killing their motivation right from the beginning. You really want a career path laid out so someone can go from being an apprentice to eventually becoming an owner of their own company. Some people want to be their own boss.

---

[3] Also, always pay your employees on time so they're never going to have to ask for their pay.

For team members who want to have their own company one day, this can be a great opportunity for both your company and them. Each year, get clear on each of your team's life and career goals and how you can help them accomplish their goals (as they help you build yours).

So, if your foreman wants his own business, here's what you can do:

1. Get clear on the timeline; when does he want to do it? 12, 24, or 36 months from now?

2. Outline the skills he needs to learn to make this a success:

    o   Read plans

    o   Run client meetings

    o   Hold construction meetings

    o   Forecast labour by stage

    o   Price projects accurately

    o   Backcost in real time

    o   Run toolbox meetings

    o   And so on…

3. Make a quarterly plan for him to learn these skills and implement all these systems into your business, thus strengthening his skills and your business.

4. Then, if he's a good fit for another location for your business, you could open up a 50/50 partnership.

BUILDER'S ROADMAP TIP:

GET THE MOST OUT OF YOUR APPRENTICES BY TRUSTING THEM WITH IMPORTANT TASKS.

As opposed to going to University, coming out with a degree, and having a $40,000+ loan, your apprentices are learning on the job. It's crucial for them to understand and constantly refer back to why they're doing the apprenticeship in the first place—especially the young guys. What's the goal? They're not going to buy a boat or a car; they're actually there to learn the trade (and it's really awesome when your apprentice can look up to your foreman who is getting a good bonus, driving a nice car, and living in a nice house).

Because it's not all about the money with your apprentices, their time with you should centre around good training. You want to make sure they're going to be highly sought after when they finish their apprenticeships. For this to happen, make sure your foreman who's in charge on site knows how to actually get the best out of them. There's no point in the foreman just having the apprentice dig holes all day as busy work. If you need your apprentice to dig holes, that's fine, but allow them to do tasks beyond the basic ones so they can learn. In this example, once he's dug the hole, let the apprentice put the timber pile in, put the joints on, and help lay the floor. This gives him a bit of light at the end of the tunnel in terms of learning the trade.

If you can get your employees/contractors running a job acting like it's their company, taking that level of professionalism, ownability, and accountability for it, you're going to make way more profit. This is especially true of your foreman, who is going to help save you labour hours. When your foreman has ownership of their job, he's naturally going to perform better, control the job better on the way through, and work hard to keep your top guys involved.

Approaching training this way gives everyone on the team a feeling of belonging. Everyone's looking towards the same goal. Then, you, as the business owner, are going to make more profit as you have a better-skilled team taking ownership and responsibility for the company. It all starts with things like having a young apprentice of two years running a small bathroom job. You've got to upskill them, train them, and give them a pathway to follow. This will allow them to grow in their desire and ability to own their own business and because of this, you'll be able to hold their interest for years to come. The only way you're going to build a culture of people who want to stay with your company is to invest in them with your knowledge and experience. And if you invest in your team members, they will invest in you.

> *The processes we have in place for our team are what we learned from TPB. We have daily logs and team incentives. Each team member has clearly defined roles and responsibilities, from the laborer to the foreman. They follow it, and they love it.*

> –David W, Hanmer Springs

BUILDER'S ROADMAP TIP:

IMPROVE COMPANY CULTURE BY PLANNING FUN THINGS TOGETHER EVERY 90 DAYS.

Building rapport with your team allows you to grow and scale. Everyone on the team is on the same page. Business is a team sport, and winning together feels great.

Every three months, do a social activity—whether it's go-karting, barbecuing, or playing pool—with your team. Activities like this keep the team together. People naturally socialise on the job, but obviously, they're working, so building a really good close-knit building company with great culture means being able to share some outside time together as well. Incentives aren't always money. You can even give days off.

MAINTAIN A WORK ENVIRONMENT CONDUCIVE TO PROGRESS

It's best to match up the right kind of people to do the right kind of work. Do you have your foreman going out to get the coffee? Your foreman should be focusing on their specialty. You're going to want your apprentice doing that. Who's doing the demo work? Is it your young guys, your hammerhands, your apprentices, or is it some of your more experienced builders? Who's filling up the jumbo bin? Always match your labour to the skill set of what's needed on site.

When it comes to apprentices, they start at zero, so they need to be trained in everything. As you go through their apprenticeships and their trade qualifications, you can look at all their work and see where they're at. Having regular meetings with them will let you know exactly what areas they're lacking in and need to improve on.

WHEN TO HIRE/PROMOTE BASED ON YOUR BMD

Systemise yourself out of the lower-dollar-value, repetitive tasks, or stuff that is below your pay grade. For you, that might be pricing, project management, or doing payroll. If you set a deadline for the task you need to stop doing. This way, you have time to set up the systems required and train the person or hire the right person who can do the tasks for you. For example:

"My last day on project managing will be.."

"My last day on pricing will be…"

"My last day on emailing clients will be…"

Now, you'll want to train or hire more than just one person in a role; you want to have people cross-trained. They'll still have their specialties, but in case any of the team is away, then someone else can still take over and do that task. It's not reliant upon you being pulled back in to the day to day.

To make this work smoothly, you want to put the name of the person who currently does that particular task. So if you're the project manager, put your name there. If you're doing the estimating or the pricing, put your name there. Maybe you hate estimating, and you're at the stage where it makes sense to outsource that.

Work with your team for the next six to eight weeks to get consistent estimating at the right price, pricing to a target gross margin, and over-head recovery margin, and include a project management fee. The next key step is to line that up with your cash flow forecast so you can hire that person with confidence that you've got enough money in the bank account to pay for that person. Typically you'll take that person on when you have at least six months' worth of their salary sitting in the bank.

INTRODUCING NEW PEOPLE AS YOU CLIMB THE BUILDER'S LADDER

Train and elevate your project manager or foreman to be doing your weekly meetings with clients and construction meetings, *so you don't have to*. A great way to introduce this as part of your sales process is to have a document to show clients who and how each person will be involved in the process. Here's an excerpt from one of our members' Pre-Construction documents:

> "This is John. He's your onsite foreman, and he will be responsible for discussing any change orders/variations you want done."

> "This is Steve, our PM/QS. He will be on-site once per week to keep you informed and answer any questions."

> "This is Mary from marketing. She will be in contact each month to see how everything is going and to take photos and videos of your project."

> "This is Brendan. He's the owner of the company and will be overseeing your project throughout the build."

HOW TO PREPARE FOR A NEW HIRE

When it's time to bring in someone new, be clear on who you want to hire and what the job entails. Communicate this to that person right off the bat in the job posting and in interviews. Respect the process of finding the right person and feel out their vibe. The following are some tips on hiring a great team member:

1. Attract the best team. You want to position yourself as the go-to building company for top talent. Knowing what your values are for a certain role within your company and finding out if a job candidate aligns with those values during their first interview is crucial. You must also have a clear job description[4] and scorecard and make sure the person can realistically meet the criteria.

2. When hiring a new person, first and foremost, work out how much money you will need. Typically, you want to have six months' worth of salary in the bank when hiring a new team member. So if you have, let's say, an estimator that you want to hire next, and they're going to be earning $100,000 per annum, make sure you've got $50,000 in the bank *before* you hire them. If you don't have six months' salary set aside, the money could be made very quickly by hiring the right person who will bring you the profits you are planning on making. This is why it's important to have systems in place to do what you intend and really do some soul-searching when deciding whether or not to hire someone.

3. After you've got a short list of candidates, work through a three-step hiring process. Firstly, have a phone interview to sort the chaff from the wheat. Next, you'll conduct an in-person interview (these will often be done as group interviews) to assess the person against

---

[4] You can create your job descriptions based on your Stop Doing list for each role you were doing before you began delegating.

the scorecard for the role. Lastly, reference check and skills test with a half day trial.

4. Once you have found the right person to join your team who fits the Job Description, it's important you dial in clear roles, responsibilities, and expectations. Give them exact instructions so they know exactly what is expected of them. Do your research to find out what the steps are to do each task correctly in this role. Map it out, step by step. Make it foolproof. This is the system that team members will follow to ensure as few mistakes as possible.

5. Keep track of your team's performance by conducting an Employee Performance Review. This will ensure they hit their Key Performance Indicators (KPIs) and the milestones that you stated at the beginning of the hiring process. This should be based on the scorecard for that role.

MAKE IT HARD TO FAIL

Once someone works for you, whether they've been working for you for a long time or were recently hired, they need clear systems for how to do their job.

JOB EXPECTATIONS AND OBJECTIVES

APPRENTICE CARPENTER PERSONAL APPEARANCE AND CONDUCT

- Ensure your own appearance is tidy.

- Conduct a helpful and polite manner with other staff, sub trades and clients.

- Ensure steel capped boots have no steel showing through or rips/ tears.

- Ensure no smoking occurs inside any building on IB sites.

- No swearing in front of client, Project Managers, Insurers, Architects or Engineers.

STAFF WORK HOURS AND BREAKS

- Start times may vary in accordance with Duties involved onsite, general site Hours are from 7.30am to 5pm Monday to Thursday and 7.30am to 4pm Friday.

- Take regular, rest breaks during the working day.

- IB is legally obliged to allow a minimum of two paid 10-minute rest breaks and one unpaid 30-minute meal break if the work period is six to eight hours long.

- DO NOT skip breaks in order to leave early as this leads to increased fatigue which creates more hazards.

- Expectation for all IB staff to be onsite at least 5-10 minutes before work to prepare.

TOOL REQUIREMENTS

Hand Tools

- Chisels
- Square
- Roofing Square
- Level
- Apron
- Hammer
- Punches
- String line
- Chalk line

- Ruler
- Spade
- Shovel

Power Tools (To be built up by end of apprenticeship)

- Circular Saw
- Nail Gun - Gas/Battery Type
- Battery Drill
- Battery Impact Driver
- Electric Planer
- Teck screw driver bits (IB to replace once worn out)

PPE

- Ear Muffs
- Safety Glasses (IB to replace as required)
- Safety Boots (IB will replace on annual basis – allowance of $100)

Record Keeping

- Hours kept for each day and including a brief summary of tasks.

Health and Safety

- Ensure you sign in and out of site each time you arrive or exit site.
- Make sure you are fully aware of emergency assembly points and emergency procedures.
- You will make sure you ask for an induction for each site you work at

- You will ensure a High vis vest/clothing are worn at all times

- Correct PPE worn when required, set a good example to all apprentices

- Assist Site managers to identify hazards, mitigate these immediately using the Eliminate, Isolate, Minimise management structure. Assist site managers with writing up all hazards on the hazard board.

- Ensure you are working to a Task analysis for the job you are completing.

- Take part in tool box talks weekly, make a point to run these occasionally to support the site manager.

- Fill in the incident/accident register whenever you have an accident or near miss.

- Ensure all IB power tools you use and your own gear have up to date Tags, 3 monthly.

- Assist site manager in completing the site inspection report occasionally. These can be done by any trained carpenter or apprentice at the site managers discretion.

- Read and understand the Health and Safety Policies and SSSP.

Key Expectations

- Listen carefully and carry out duties given to you by your site Forman

- Ask questions for anything you are not sure about.

- Work diligently and courteously to carry out the task.

- Let the Site manager know of any materials that are running in short supply so more can be ordered.

- Support the Site manger as much as you can.

- When required by your site manager there is an expectation in this company to help out as much as you can, be flexible, work later on occasion as deadlines may need to be met.

IB preferential items to assist you getting pay rises, (courses done at your own cost):

- Assist Site Managers in Meeting Deadlines, work hard.
- Read all your theory notes, complete all worksheet exercises
- Put your name forward for Health and Safety Representative roles (for senior apprentices)
- Ask "what can I do to be more involved with Health and Safety" and get delegated some responsibility.
- Be solutions focused – Proactive not reactive.
- Get your NZ certificate in Carpentry
- Obtain some higher level Site Safe Training, Gold Card, Supervisor courses
- Obtain a current 2 day Comprehensive First Aid Course
- Obtain a forklift licence
- Obtain Wheel, Tracks and Rollers if this interests you
- Read more books with any aspect helpful to construction and people management:
  o Leadership
  o Construction Techniques

Also (and this one's a biggie), *everyone* on your team should know where the systems for each part of your business are kept. When it comes to handbooks, training, and system information, keep them all in one place where they can be easily accessed by those who need them. You can start with Google Drive to create them and eventually move to a platform like SystemsHub. You can upload a Loom training video there and put a questionnaire after it if you want them to answer any questions to ensure trainees understand what they've watched. They can also tick training they've reviewed already. Get people on the same page, whether it's in digital, physical, or video form.

> *"TPB systems helped my team to step up. I decided to go on a 6-week vacation to Europe, but I was concerned things would go under. Turns out, my team just signed [two] new jobs. And when I got back, everything was handled perfectly."*
>
> –Alvin C, Bombay

ENFORCE THESE SYSTEMS WITH MEETINGS AND KPIS

The way you establish trust and verify that everyone's doing their job well is to have regular weekly meetings. As a profitable builder, you'll need four main meetings to start (we'll talk about the other three big ones in a bit—seven in total):

1. A management meeting

2. A construction meeting

3. A marketing/sales meeting

4. Toolbox meeting

…with *all* team members involved in each project to see exactly how each department of your business is doing. You want to be asking the right questions at each of these meetings:

- *Is the project on track?* (Use and check those KPIs and KPAs)

- How are we doing with materials?

- Are we capturing all the contract variations?

- Is labour on track to hit the next milestone for the next progress payment?
- How are we doing in terms of forecast vs actual hours so we can get within 5% of the labour hours forecast?

There needs to be a specific agenda for each of these core meetings. If you've already got them in place, fantastic. They should all have a stop time and a start time. If you don't have a stop time, they'll just run and run. They also need an agenda. So, what is the format going to be? Write it down and have it ready to reference each time you run a meeting/have management or a foreman run it for you. Consistency is what will make each meeting shorter, smoother, and more efficient.

KNOW AND SHOW YOUR NUMBERS—AS OFTEN AS POSSIBLE

Each meeting needs metrics. As previously mentioned, each team member should be assigned no more than three KPAs with one KPI.

> "When I first joined TPB, I thought meetings were a waste of time. In my mind, I thought we could do something more productive than just sitting around. But then I implemented the process I learned from you guys, and the team has been loving it. It gives us a sense of direction of where we are heading."
>
> —Jon F, Texas

What you measure gets managed, and you need to know and show your numbers weekly (don't wait a full month to get your numbers). During these meetings, you can write your metrics on a whiteboard or display them on a TV screen/monitor.

Track numbers daily and display them at daily stand-up meetings[5]. Slackbot is good for getting feedback from your team members on how to improve these numbers.

YOUR TWO-WEEK SPRINT MEETINGS

You need a plan—a routine. And you've got to give *one* routine an honest try before you decide to move on and try another. What I'm going to give you now is an effective routine for you to execute every two weeks, where you'll check in weekly to see where you're at in the cycle. It's helped the top construction businesses increase their productivity and profit, so if you follow exactly what's laid out here, you won't need another routine. We call this the Two-Week Sprint, and each week have a Two-Week Sprint Meeting to make sure you're on track before, during, and after this two-week period.

> *"Systems [are] one of the biggest things Marti helped us with. I used to have no systems, and running the business was like swimming in a pond of oil. But now everything is structured, every job has project management and is tracked properly."*
>
> –Rowan C, Auckland

A Two-Week Sprint is a two-week period in which the team is focused on improving one particular area of the business that needs a boost of productivity. Choose the focus of each Two-Week Sprint based on your current red-light items from your A-Z of Operations.

---

[5] Short organisational meetings held daily (they can be held in the afternoon at the end of the workday)

1. THE ONE-PAGE BUSINESS PLAN

Once you're clear on the particular areas of your business that need to be solved (start with the red-light stuff), you can project where you want your business to be in the future as a team. At your first Two-Week Sprint Meeting, answer the following questions as a team:

1. What are our one-year, three-year, and five-year goals for this area?
2. What are the business's strengths and weaknesses in this area?
3. What is the best strategy for this area to implement for where the company is at right now?
4. What does success look like with that strategy?
5. How will we execute that strategy?

Once you know the answers to these questions, write them down. This way, you can start charting out your **One-Page Business Plan**, a valuable tool for getting your goals clear to move in the right direction. At your next Two-Week Sprint Meeting, assess where you are as a team in relation to these goals. Here's our sheet for organising this clearly:

TPB | THE PROFESSIONAL BUILDER | 1-PAGE BUSINES PLAN

START DATE:	
CORE VALUES:	PSR → Problem, Solution, Recommendation Speed of Execution World Class
PURPOSE - WHY WE DO THIS:	Be the best and build a world class business that changes lives
AREA YOU DO WORK IN:	Christchurch
TARGET MARKET - TYPE OF JOBS YOU SPECIALISE IN:	Architectural New Builds & Renovations $200k+

BUSINESS MATURITY DATE (BMD) - LONG TERM GOAL OF WHAT WE WILL ACHIEVE

	Now	90-Days	12 Months	3 Years
Salary You Pay Yourself:	$96,000	$96,000	$145,000	$300,000
Net Profit Your Business Makes:	$150,000	$182,000	$260,000	$600,000
Days You Take Off A Month:	10	11	15	
Holidays You Take Annually:	2 Weeks		6 weeks	10 Weeks
Person In charge of Sales & Marketing:	Me	New S&M Coordinator		
Person In charge of Project Management:	John			
Person In charge of Admin & Accounts:	Me	New admin help		
Person In charge of Pricing & Estimating:	Me	Me/ Software	Me	QS
Who Will You Hire Next & When?:	Admin help			

WHAT WILL BE MY REWARD FOR ACHIEVING THESE TARGETS AND GOALS?

Lambo + Hublot Watch

STRATEGIC MOVES - TO BE IMPLEMENTED WITHIN THE NEXT 3-5 YEARS:

1. Do 2x Developments
2. Achieve Business Maturity Date
3. Set up Second Location

THE PROFITABLE BUILDER'S PLAYBOOK

KPI TARGETS AND MILESTONES (MONTHLY)

Metric (MONTHLY)	Now	In 90-Days Time	In 12 Months Time
Number of Leads Generated That Meet Your Criteria:	8	8	12
Conversion Rate of Number of Priced Jobs to Signed Contracts/Deposit Secured:	25%	33%	50%
Average Project value:	$150,000	$200,000	$400,000
Gross Profit % From Last Month:	15%	17%	22%
Operators Salary You Pay Yourself Monthly:	$8,000	$8,000	$12,000
Fixed Costs Monthly (Expenses Including your Operators Salary):	$20,000	$22,000	$25,000
Net Profit Monthly:	$12,500	$14,000	$20,000
How many days off in the last Month:	10	11	15
Hours Per Week - An average from the last Month:	55	50	40

[CLICK HERE TO Use The TPB Forecasting Tool]

PRIMARY METRIC TO IMPROVE - THE BIGGEST OPPORTUNITY TO IMPROVE YOUR BUSINESS IS?

Margin up from 17% to 22%

CURRENT OPPORTUNITIES	CURRENT THREATS
Hire foreman - Get pricing software	Competing on price and operating at low margins

CURRENT STRENGTHS	CURRENT WEAKNESSES
Team Quality of Work	Marketing KPI's Through Website

1 YEAR STRATEGIC PLANNING BY QUARTER:	Q1	Q2	Q3	Q4
	Sales	Marketing	Operations/Site	Pricing

90 DAY STRATEGIC PRIORITIES:

- Improve back end margin on current jobs
- Attract larger sized leads and projects
- Refine sales process to sort out tyre kickers

PROJECT PLANS TO ACHIEVE PRIORITIES:

- Complete 27 Tips to make more profit checklist
- Complete video testimonials of our big projects
- Connect with our Dream 10 Architects & Partners and offer them the TPB 1% Referral Process
- Set sales script to qualify time wasters

2. THE 90-DAY PLAN

Once you've got the strategy, the next key part is to reduce overwhelm and speed up execution. To do this, you need a 90-Day Plan. When planning the next 90 days with your team, it's great to go somewhere off-site so everyone is focused.

Do team reviews first thing in the morning:

Every 90 days, do your team reviews. Work out whether the team is working in alignment with your culture and your values and whether they have improved on what they needed to work on in the last 90 days. This is where you can evaluate your team's Scorecards.

See how your team stacks up every 90 days. Remember to plan out the following 90-day meeting date (90 days from the first Two-Week Sprint meeting) and let everyone know when that is.

1. **Work out what the core tasks are for the next 90 days according to the team review:** Put these core tasks up on the whiteboard. Then, ask the group, "Out of the 20 or 30 things we could do, what are the top five that are going to make the most difference?"

2. **Identify commonalities among the top five most chosen ones:** The last step will give you a list of what the top five projects to work on should be. Now, the number of projects that you can take on in a 90-day slot depends on how many team members you have and whether or not you're working day to day in the business. For example, we've got 47 people, so we can take on a reasonable number of projects (typically one major project per team member on the management team).

3. **Work out the logistics of each core task:** Figure out what you need to **stop** doing to accomplish them and what you should **continue** doing. Then look at what you need to **start** doing.

4. **Disperse the microtasks involved:** Spread all the sub-tasks across each Two-Week Sprint within the 90-day slot, complete with assigned roles, KPIs, and KPAs for each one. Write the dates for each Two-Week Sprint period moving forward and pair it with a smaller task that was worked out when you were doing your plan. This will also include the tasks you need to stop doing.

5. **Examine your business as a whole:** Take a look at your marketing, sales, systems, pricing, operations, team, and financials. Pick out which areas you need to focus on in comparison to the previous 90 days and repeat. Perhaps you need to focus on improving your cash flow, reducing your debtors, or putting better systems in place on site to hit project milestones and improve cashflow and quality.

3. ICE

Upon discovering the things you need to start doing in your business every 90 days, run each task through the ICE Scoring Model.

ICE is a fantastic way to make accurate decisions. Upon analysing each task, ask the group:

- How much **Impact** is this going to have? How much will it move the needle? Creating an info pack for your sales process, for example, is going to make a massive difference, so that might get a nine. Improving your contract variations process may get a seven if your team is missing them.

- How **Certain** are you that you can get this into play? Have you done it before? Is there a template you can use? Is there another builder who's done it successfully you can talk to? Perhaps with the task of creating an info pack, your confidence level is at a seven. Establishing a contract variations process is more straightforward, so that might be a nine.

- What's the **Ease of Execution** for completing this task? The variations process might be a seven and the info pack a four. The higher **Ease** score means the task is going to be quicker to get into play.

Strategy	Impact (1-10)	Certainty (1-10)	Ease of Execution (1-10)	Total Score
Look Book	5	5	8	18
Office Manager	8	8	8	24
Scorecards	8	6	5	19
PM Software	8	6	4	18

I.C.E Framework.
It works by giving your shortlist of strategies a score you can use to prioritise what to work on first.

Impact
What will the impact of this strategy be on my time, savings, and profits?
1 = Suck, 10 = Off to retirement

Certainty
By doing this strategy I'm certain the desired result will happen?
1 = You're Dreaming, 10 = I'm a true believer, drinking the kool-aid

Ease of Execution
Will this take much of my time, team's time, or our resources?
1 = Time and money pit, 10 = Low/No operational overhead

The task that gets the highest of these scores becomes your number one strategy for your first Two-Week Sprint, and the next highest ones would be the focus of their respective Two-Week Sprints thereafter until that 90-day period is up.

Now, what are the steps to make this task happen? What's the outcome? What does success look like? Who's going to be involved? What are the milestones? And when will it be done?

4. THE FIVE W'S AND ONE H

Once you've chosen your projects, decide who's going to own each one. Each project should have a:

- Who?
- What?
- When?
- Where?
- Why?
- How?

The person who has a project then breaks it down into smaller tasks that they're going to do for that Two-Week Sprint according to these answers. This is where your values for each individual role, along with its KPIs, come in.

TOOLBOX MEETINGS

As the residential construction company owner, you need to break the process down by stage to control your labour on site. Your foremen should have a very clear understanding of what has to happen and ensure the team follows suit, so holding weekly Toolbox Meetings is crucial.

The foreman's got one job: make sure the project gets done efficiently and effectively. They have the plans and they help with the pricing, so they've got to have accountability throughout the job.

Your foremen should be running the Toolbox Meetings with the team on site. Make sure these meetings happen weekly. The following sheet is an agenda that covers what should be discussed at the Toolbox Meeting.

TOOLBOX MEETING

AGENDA

Date: 16th October

Start Time: 7:30 AM

Venue: Site Office – 123 Elm Street

Attendees:

John Smith – Site Manager

Liam Davies – Apprentice

Rebecca Green – Project Manager

David Taylor – Foreman

Tom Harris – Labourer

HEALTH & SAFETY

HAZARDS/NEAR MISSES:

- *Tripping hazards* around the building foundation. Materials to be stacked properly to avoid accidents.
- *Near miss* on scaffolding yesterday: incorrect access route. Ensure ladders are secured and the proper path is used.

STATS:

- 14 days without a reportable incident.
- 1 safety breach last week (non-use of safety harness).

RULES OF THE GAME – VISION (REMINDER)

"Build quality homes, safely and on schedule."

- *Shout out*: David for quick problem-solving during the foundation pour delay.
- *Brag*: Liam for showing improvement in his formwork skills.

JOB STATUS

ACTUAL TO BUDGET:

- *Current Job Status*: $270,000 spent, tracking well against the $300,000 allocated for this stage of the build.

WEEKS FORECAST:

- Focus for the next two weeks: Completing external cladding and roof framing.

VARIATIONS:

- Client requested a variation for an additional deck off the living room. This will add 3 days to the project timeline.

ISSUES:

- Delay in material delivery (timber for roof trusses) expected on Thursday.
- Water seepage on-site due to heavy rain – plan to pump out water from the foundation by midweek.

QUALITY:

- No defects reported, but team to ensure all framing is checked twice to avoid rework.
- External cladding work needs closer attention to detail – some panels misaligned.

TIME LOGGING:

- Reminder: Time sheets to be submitted by Friday morning.
- Supervisors to ensure all apprentices are accurately logging time spent on each task.

DAY BY DAY OVERVIEW:

- **Monday:** Finalise formwork for footings.
- **Tuesday**: Begin wall framing on the southern side of the building.
- **Wednesday**: Continue cladding preparation.
- **Thursday**: Install roof trusses (pending material arrival).
- **Friday**: Finish external framing.

HOUSEKEEPING

- All excess building materials must be stacked neatly by the site entrance to avoid blocking access.
- Ensure tools are returned to the tool shed after each use, especially shared power tools.
- Rubbish bins for recycling and general waste to be emptied daily to prevent overflow.

INITIATIVES (CONTINUOUS IMPROVEMENT)

- Trial a new scheduling app for better team coordination on-site.
- Set up a system for early identification of material shortages to prevent delays.

REVIEWS – FEEDBACK

- John: "We need to keep better track of deliveries. Some materials have gone missing and caused delays."
- David: "The new apprentice training sessions are really helping – would be good to focus more on health & safety procedures."
- Tom: "The site layout could be better organised, too much walking around for tools."

GENERAL BUSINESS

- *Weather forecast* shows rain for the next few days, ensure tarps are available to protect the timber frame.
- *Next toolbox meeting* to be scheduled for Friday, 23rd October.

GIVE YOUR FOREMAN OWNERSHIP OF THE PROJECT

The QS/estimator prices the job, but the foreman should also price the labour so he is more personally invested in working efficiently. Have him sit in the office for three to five hours to prepare, plan, and estimate the labour. Especially when you've secured a more demanding job that's more involved or that's been quoted at a higher price. Get your foreman in early to do an estimation of the labour before the project is secured. This estimation doesn't include the materials; it's purely for the labour hours. You give your foreman the plans, and they'll have to study them and come back to you with a breakdown by stage.

Let them know the specific areas you want them to look at and really allow them time at work to do this properly. The foreman shouldn't be doing this on their own time. If you say, "Go home and do homework," they won't want to do it. They've got kids and their own things going on. So it's unrealistic to expect them to do the planning during the time they'd rather be spending in other ways—time they're not getting paid for.

In addition to having the foreman take ownership of their job, it's a good idea to have either your QS, your Project Manager, or yourself look at the job as well so they can compare notes. Then both of you can go through the drawings together as a great opportunity for you to learn the intricacies of the job. If you go through the details of the job to work out the labour for framing or interior linings, and then he does the same, you might go, "Well, hey, I had 85 hours for the framing. Why have you got 110? I had 95 hours for the interior linings. You've only got 83. Why?" This process will help you develop better synergy, and over three or four jobs, you're going to get a lot more clarity and a lot closer to your actual labour hours.

Your foreman's got a huge responsibility, so reward him with good bonuses that come from the labour that is saved by his labour estimations and efficiency on the job. If you have three guys on site doing 40 hours a week for a fixed-price contract job, and you are billing them out at, say, $60 an hour, it would be 120 labour hours, so that's $7,200 per week. If you can get the foreman to drive and control the job by incentivising him with 20% of the labour saved, you've just saved one week's labour; you've just saved $7,200! The foreman gets $1,440 of that, and you've just made an extra $5,760. Now, not only have you done that, but you've also got another week's labour and finished that project early.

If the foreman can go, "I own this job. This is my job," and they can see their bonuses, they are properly incentivised to make sure the project hits the milestones, and forecast labour hours by stage and quality levels.

> *"I stopped trying to do everything on-site and let my foreman be in charge. Instead of taking over, I set targets for them and push them to hit them. Having the A - Z Of Operations and on-site checklists makes it ten times easier."*
>
> –David S, Texas

SCHEDULING MEETINGS AND TASKS

It doesn't matter what day of the week you schedule these meetings. All that matters is that they happen every week at the same time, with the same agenda and action points.

Remember to stick to your Default Diary of tasks you need to do. Give your team members Default Diaries of their own and let their work tasks flow from yours—the ones you don't have time to do. Here's an example of the Default Diary of an Office Manager:

Daily Schedule for Office Admin

Time	Task
8:00 AM – 9:00 AM	**Morning Financial Tasks**
	Check Invoices: Review client payments and accounts receivable from the previous day.
	Bank Transfers: Process any necessary payments or transfers.
	QuickBooks, Hubdoc, Data Entry: Input any new financial data from the previous day.
9:00 AM – 10:00 AM	**Team Time Management**
	Track Employee Time: Enter employee timesheets, track sick days, holidays, and approve requests.
	Payroll Prep: If it's payroll week, review and enter payroll details.
10:00 AM – 10:15 AM	**Email and Communication Check**
	Check emails for urgent matters, communications from the owner, and client follow-ups.
	Follow up on payments: Send out any reminders for overdue invoices.
10:15 AM – 11:00 AM	**Financial Management**
	Assist Owner with Financial Tasks: Meet with the owner (if needed) to assist with any financial decision-making or strategy discussions.
	Prepare Monthly Profit/Loss/Cashflow Reports (if it's close to the end of the month).
11:00 AM – 12:00 PM	**HR and Employee Management**
	Employee Claims: Manage any WorksafeBC or employee claims.
	Holiday and Leave Management: Update holiday and sick day balances for employees.
	Document Employee Onboarding: If any new employees are being onboarded, ensure contracts and paperwork are in order.
12:00 PM – 1:00 PM	**Lunch Break**
1:00 PM – 2:00 PM	**Administrative and Document Management**
	Systemize and Document Office Processes: Create or update SOPs for any office tasks or processes.
	Organize Filing and Google Drive: Ensure all important documents are filed correctly (both digitally and physically).
	Review Company Licenses and Subscriptions: Check and renew any upcoming licenses or insurance.
2:00 PM – 3:00 PM	**Marketing Support**
	Website Management: Update the company website as needed.
	Assist with Creation of Marketing Materials: Help design or review any new marketing collateral (social media posts, blog posts, client proposals).
3:00 PM – 3:30 PM	**Prepare for Tomorrow**
	Prepare Tomorrow's Tasks: Create a to-do list for the next day based on pending tasks or upcoming deadlines.
	Email Wrap-Up: Check emails again and respond to any outstanding communications.
3:30 PM – 4:00 PM	**Follow Up on Payments and Client Requests**
	Payment Follow-Up: Follow up with clients regarding outstanding invoices and check for any new client inquiries.
4:00 PM – 4:30 PM	**Final Check and Wrap Up**
	Final Check on Invoices and Payroll: Ensure all financial entries are up to date.
	Office Tidy and File Organization: Take a few minutes to tidy the workspace and ensure everything is organized.

For larger views of the tables featured in this book, scan the QR code at the end of each chapter to access a complete list of resources and images.

Even if you don't have all of these roles filled yet, it's worth the time to plan out this stage of the task-scheduling process. What would your Project Manager's Default Diary look like? What would your Estimator or your QS's Default Diary look like? What about your foremen?

THE BEST WAY TO GET THE MONKEY OFF YOUR BACK

Part of training your team is teaching them how to communicate with management. They need to be proactive in coming up with their own solutions so they can become more and more self-sufficient as time goes on. This will help amplify your trust in them. As you begin to take hours, days, weeks, or ultimately even months off, you can rest assured that they can solve problems effectively. It's not your job to do their job; your job is to help them become better problem solvers. The problem-solving framework we give our members is called PSR. When a team member comes to you with an issue, follow these steps:

1. **Problem**: Have them clearly define the problem, down to the specific stage in the system that they're having the problem in.

2. **Solutions**: Have them give you 3 possible solutions they came up with on their own.

3. **Recommendation**: Have them pick the best solution and explain why they chose it.

…and let go. Trust that this team member wants to do well. Offer all of the expertise you can, but don't do their job for them. Help them help themselves, and just gently course-correct them if you see they're about to get off course.

Trust but verify. Inspect what you expect.

Leading a successful team will make you a better leader. As you can see, all of these systems you'll be using with your team are there to:

Save **Y**ou **S**tress, **T**ime, **E**nergy, & **M**oney

Now, as we go into Part 2 of the book, you'll learn how to hone in on the smaller details that will have big implications for your profit margin and your abilities as a profitable building company owner. You'll gain the confidence to handle the trickier parts of owning a construction company and be well on your way to becoming more profitable—enough to get those 8 hours back in the next 90 days!

ACTION STEPS

1. Meet with each team member to get clear on what their personal success looks like. Then align it with the company's goals so everyone wins together.

2. Everyone needs the following to be set and agreed on:

   - Job Description

   - Key Performance Indicators (KPIs) and Key Performance Areas (KPAs)

   - Scorecard

   - Perfect Week (Default Diary)

   - Weekly Meetings

   - Quarterly Evaluation

   - Incentives

Scan the code for all the resources

MEMBER PROFILE: ADAM C.

When I first met Adam, he was just starting his building company and wanted to start off with strong systems and have them in place early. But he was spinning too many plates.

On weekends, his phone rang relentlessly from clients wanting to go over projects. He buried himself with paperwork in the evenings and barely had time to spend with his family. He was just one step away from burning out.

And since his business was young, he competed on price to win jobs. His prospects would consistently haggle over the price, and Adam was forced to cut his price because he needed to keep his guys busy.

Get paid what you are worth.

He was sick and tired of getting paid pennies on the dollar. He wanted someone to point him in the right direction.

When Adam found us on Facebook and decided to join The Professional Builder, we rolled up our sleeves and started structuring his daily schedule and the team so he could focus on his zone of genius: estimating projects.

We set clear job descriptions and KPIs for his two assistant project managers to ensure all materials, timelines, and quality of work were on point.

He also implemented the Default Diary and weekly structure with his construction manager to get progress updates on project milestones and made sure they were on top of their tasks.

Next, we dialled in his sales system, the qualifying questionnaire, and pricing for profit. These processes helped Adam weed out time wasters and secure projects with gross margins above 20%.

After a year, Adam went to Europe for 2 weeks without checking his emails. He also increased his turnover from $850,000 to $3.2M with a healthy gross profit margin. Right now, Adam has no trouble finding high-value clients. In fact, he's booked out 6-12 months in advance with profitable jobs

1. Marti & Owen recording another podcast episode on who to hire, when, & how so you keep your company profitable whilst buying back your time.

2. Matt Fenn, from Hawke's Bay, New Zealand, & Marti working through his next hire for his BMD (Business Maturity Date).

3. Taki Moore, Marti, Owen winning 'The Blade' for best coaching business at Taki Moore's Boardroom event in Newport Beach, California, USA.

4. Marti on stage at Gold Coast, Australia, 2-day summit, training members on profit strategies in a mastermind roundtable where members share their best tactics of what's working right now for them.

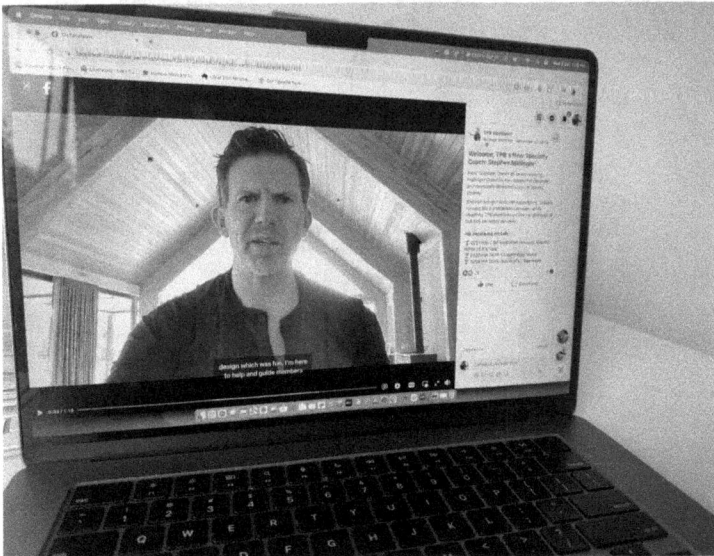

5. Stephen Mallinger from Mallinger Construction, Sydney, Australia, one of our specialty coaches, running through his cost-plus contracts & process for projects $1m+.

6. Some of our top-performing TPB members at the Builders Summit on the Gold Coast, where we celebrated their hard work and results. Matt Fenn, Justin Cook, and Brad & Dan Boersma were among those recognized for their outstanding progress in building systemised, profitable businesses.

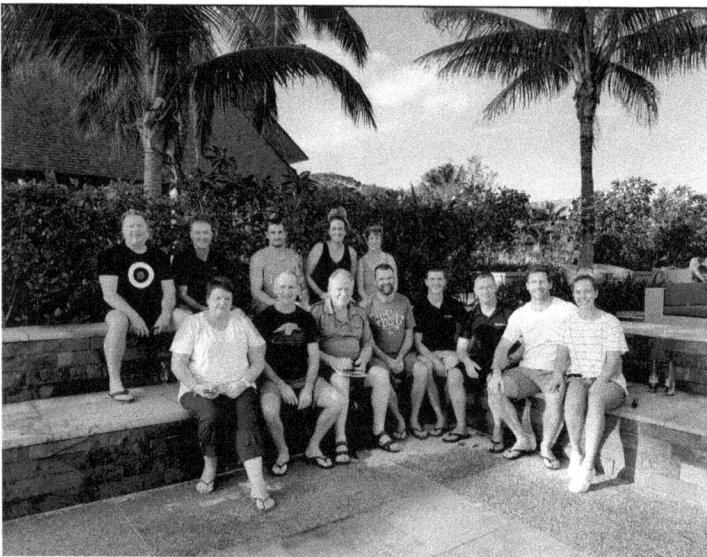

7. TPB Fiji Boardroom intensive. Every year, TPB holds in-person regular events in Australia, New Zealand, USA & other exotic locations like Fiji, Canada, Bali, Philippines, & Mexico. Members come together to brainstorm, learn, network, & build lifelong friendships, whilst building a better business.

8. The TPB team representing regions from across the globe, including New Zealand, Australia, the United States, Argentina, Canada, the Philippines, Mexico, and Bali, coming together as a united force.

9. Jet boating at TPBs leadership retreat with Auckland team members.

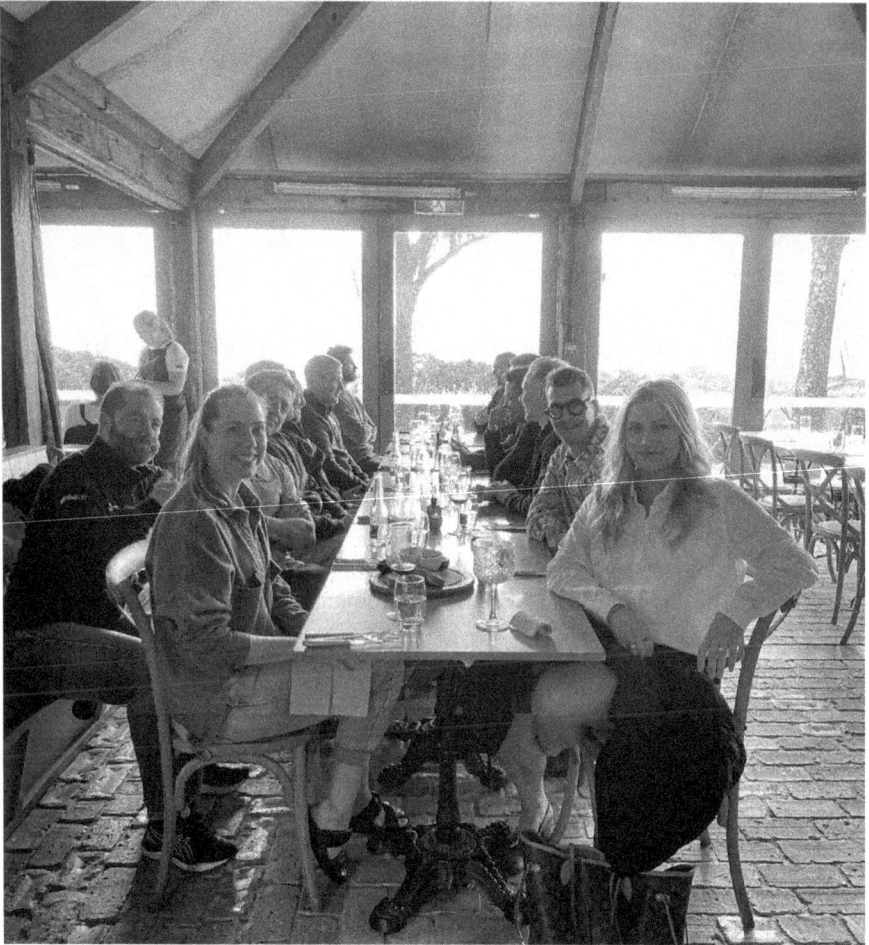

10. The Auckland team gathered at the picturesque Waiheke Island Boardroom event, collaborating and strategising for the year ahead.

11. TPB's Women in Construction Group Monthly Meetup—
our community providing connection, support,
and empowerment for female members in the building industry.

12. TPB Coaches and Members enjoying a well-earned dinner
together after a full day of learning and growth at the Gold Coast Summit.

PART ONE SUMMARY
RINSE AND REPEAT—EVERY 90 DAYS

Every 90 days, go through the processes outlined in Part 1 of this book to ensure you're working in your zone of genius. Focus on the 20% of your tasks that move the needle. Your business will look massively different 90 days from now in terms of how much you're enjoying it, and you will be making more profit.

You now know how to handle the parts of your business you were perhaps initially hesitant to manage. Part 2 is about the key functions of your business and how to make sure you understand your business as a whole so you can become the profitable building company owner you need to be to live your ideal lifestyle.

PART TWO
RUNNING YOUR BUSINESS DAILY

Part Two of this book focuses on how to run your business daily to get ahead of the top 5 challenges most residential construction company owners know all too well:

- Understanding (and thus being able to control) the numbers that drive the business
- How to price projects profitably and manage a job before, during, and after a build to stay profitable the whole way through
- Being able to consistently acquire high-quality projects
- Having a dependable sales process you can rely on
- How to set your business up for sale

At the core of *all* of these challenges is numbers.

Yes, I know. Numbers are scary because they tell the truth. Honestly, though, it's really not that bad once you're aware of those numbers and what to do about them. That's what the Builder's Roadmap is for; to show you step by step what numbers you need to track and the actions that will make your business more profitable.

The 4 Levers Business Dashboard allows you to track the most critical numbers that you can change to get better results. Throughout Part Two, I will lead you through how to get to these numbers and keep calculating them every month so your business stays on track.

CHAPTER 4 – SUMMARY
KNOW THE NUMBERS THAT DRIVE YOUR BUSINESS

Numbers are the language of business. They let you know what's working well and what to fix in your business.

- Get a monthly Profit and Loss to compare to your budget and stay on track to hit your goals

- Price to a target margin. Don't confuse markup with margin or it will keep you poor.

- Make sure you hit the golden ratios:

  o Gross Profit 20%+
  o Overheads (including owner's salary) 8%-12%
  o Net Profit 10%+

- Use the 4 Levers Profit Calculator to identify where to focus your efforts to drive the most profit.

KNOW THE NUMBERS THAT DRIVE YOUR BUSINESS

Get the facts, or the facts will get you.
And when you get 'em, get 'em right,
or they will get you wrong.
–Thomas Fuller

When I first started my business, I coached every type of business: franchises, hairdressing salons, manufacturers, mortgage broking, insurance, retail, wholesale, architects, and every type of trade, including painting, electrical, plumbing, design, landscaping and, of course, building. The ones I most enjoyed working with were trade businesses—specifically residential construction company owners. We were able to get them some huge results quickly by helping them understand the key numbers that drive cash flow and where to focus their energy for maximum profit.

Numbers tell the story of what's working well and what needs to change. Numbers show you exactly where to put your focus.

FIRST THINGS FIRST: HOW TO READ YOUR NUMBERS— UNDERSTANDING YOUR PROFIT & LOSS REPORT

Your Profit and Loss Report (P&L) is the best tool available to help you understand the health and performance of your business.

Unfortunately, 87% of businesses have this report set up incorrectly. So before we go any further, let's get clear on what to look at and how to set things up so you can read the language of business: your numbers.

Ask your accountant or pull a 12-month P&L report from Xero, Quickbooks, MYOB, or whatever financial management software you use.

The first part at the top of the page is headlined total sales, revenue, or income (depending on where you are in the world).

This is the total amount of money that your company receives. We can then break this down by project to see how profitable each one is.

Think of this as the "cost to the client."

Best practice is to break this out by project.

Profit & Loss - Revenue

REVENUE	
54 Blue Street	$ 1,000,000
17 Green Street	$ 1,390,000
109 Landmark Ave	$ 510,000
1011 Coastal Highway	$ 2,100,000
TOTAL REVENUE	**$ 5,000,000**

Next comes the section called Cost of Goods, Cost of Goods Sold (COGS), Cost of Sale (COS) or variable expenses (again, depending on where you are, these will be named differently). Consider them the "costs to you" to do each job.

This should include anything we can directly attribute to a specific project. Most of the time, it will be made up of Labour, Materials, Sub contractors, and any Preliminary and General expenses.

Profit & Loss - Cost of Goods (Variable Costs)

COGS	
54 Blue Street	$ 800,000
• Labour	
• Materials	
• Sub Trades	
• Preliminary & General	
17 Green Street	$ 1,112,000
• Labour	
• Materials	
• Sub Trades	
• Preliminary & General	
109 Landmark Ave	$ 408,000
• Labour	
• Materials	
• Sub Trades	
• Preliminary & General	
1011 Coastal Highway	$ 1,680,000
• Labour	
• Materials	
• Sub Trades	
• Preliminary & General	
TOTAL COGS	$ 4,000,000

For larger views of the tables featured in this book, scan the QR code at the end of each chapter to access a complete list of resources and images.

Below your "costs to you" (Cost of Goods) will sit your Gross Profit.

You get this number by taking the "cost to the client" and subtracting the "costs to you."

Revenue - Cost of Sale = Gross Profit

Gross Profit is the amount left over and should be thought of as the amount you have to run the business and cover all of your fixed costs/overheads, including salaries* (for the off-tools team, not those attributable to jobs), AND provide a net profit to the owner.

Each job can form its own Profit & Loss to ensure that each project is profitable. This then allows us to assess how well each project has been priced and managed in regards to variations being captured or missed, labour being within 5% of target, and back costing in real time and how well the foreman (or person responsible for daily performance) is performing.

EXAMPLE

Cost to the Client (Revenue)	$1,000,000
Cost to You (COGs)	$800,000
Gross Profit	$200,000
Gross Profit % (Margin)	20%
Overheads	8%
Net Profit	12%

These projects combined give your overall company P&L. We can then see how well each of the projects is performing and contributing to overall profitability.

From your Gross Profit, you then pay Expenses or Fixed Costs (also known as Overheads). Consider these overheads as investments made to run a business, and NOT a busy job. These include accounting, project management software, team members who provide support to multiple jobs like office and project managers, owners, estimators, coaching, and sales and marketing support. Overheads will also include vehicle running costs and lease of an office.

Profit & Loss - Expenses (Fixed Costs/Overheads)

EXPENSES	
Accountant Fees	
Advertising expenses	
Bank charges	
Coaching	
Computer	
Education & Training Expenses	
Entertainment	
Fuel	
Gifts	
Hire Purchase Charges	
Insurance expenses	
Meals and entertainment	
Motor vehicle expenses	
Land Holding block costs	
Legal Expenses	
Health & Safety	
Office Expenses	
Printing, stationery & supplies	
Recruiting Expenses	
Registration Fees	
Rent	
Repairs & Maintenance	
Software & IT	
Storage	
Staff Expenses	
Subscription	
Tools	
Travel costs	
Uncategorised Expense	
Uniforms/Clothing	
Utilities - Internet	
Utilities - Mobile Phone	
Wage Expenses	
Director Salaries	
TOTAL EXPENSES	**$ 400,000**

For larger views of the tables featured in this book, scan the QR code at the end of each chapter to access a complete list of resources and images.

Finally, you end up with what is left over…before taxes. This is your EBITDA (Earnings Before Interest Tax Depreciation and Amortisation), Net Profit, or your "business owner's bonus." In other words, your take home. Net Profit is the bonus you get for taking the risk and liability of operating a business in our industry.

REVENUE		EXPENSES	
54 Blue Street	$ 1,000,000	Accountant Fees	
17 Green Street	$ 1,390,000	Advertising expenses	
		Bank charges	
109 Landmark Ave	$ 510,000	Coaching	
1011 Coastal Highway	$ 2,100,000	Computer	
TOTAL REVENUE	**$ 5,000,000**	Education & Training Expenses	
		Entertainment	
COGS		Fuel	
54 Blue Street	**$ 800,000**	Gifts	
• Labour		Hire Purchase Charges	
• Materials		Insurance expenses	
• Sub Trades		Meals and entertainment	
• Preliminary & General		Motor vehicle expenses	
17 Green Street	**$ 1,112,000**	Land Holding block costs	
• Labour		Legal Expenses	
• Materials		Health & Safety	
• Sub Trades		Office Expenses	
• Preliminary & General		Printing, stationery & supplies	
109 Landmark Ave	**$ 408,000**	Recruiting Expenses	
• Labour		Registration Fees	
• Materials		Rent	
• Sub Trades		Repairs & Maintenance	
• Preliminary & General		Software & IT	
1011 Coastal Highway	**$ 1,680,000**	Storage	
• Labour		Staff Expenses	
• Materials		Subscription	
• Sub Trades		Tools	
• Preliminary & General		Travel costs	
		Uncategorised Expense	
		Uniforms/Clothing	
		Utilities - Internet	
		Utilities - Mobile Phone	
		Wage Expenses	
		Director Salaries	
TOTAL COGS	**$ 4,000,000**	**TOTAL EXPENSES**	**$ 400,000**
GROSS PROFIT	**$ 1,000,000**	**NET PROFIT**	**$ 600,000**

For larger views of the tables featured in this book, scan the QR code at the end of each chapter to access a complete list of resources and images.

To review this report correctly, it should be reconciled and maintained so that before the 10th of every month, you can review and track your company's performance.

REVENUE		EXPENSES	
54 Blue Street	$ 1,000,000	Accountant Fees	
17 Green Street	$ 1,390,000	Advertising expenses	
109 Landmark Ave	$ 510,000	Bank charges	
1011 Coastal Highway	$ 2,100,000	Coaching	
TOTAL REVENUE	**$ 5,000,000**	Computer	
		Education & Training Expenses	
COGS		Entertainment	
54 Blue Street	**$ 800,000**	Gifts	
• Labour		Hire Purchase Charges	
• Materials		Insurance expenses	
• Sub Trades		Meals and entertainment	
• Preliminary & General		Motor vehicle expenses	
17 Green Street	**$ 1,112,000**	Land Holding block costs	
• Labour		Legal Expenses	
• Materials		Health & Safety	
• Sub Trades		Office Expenses	
• Preliminary & General		Printing, stationery & supplies	
109 Landmark Ave	**$ 408,000**	Recruiting Expenses	
• Labour		Registration Fees	
• Materials		Rent	
• Sub Trades		Repairs & Maintenance	
• Preliminary & General		Software & IT	
1011 Coastal Highway	**$ 1,680,000**	Storage	
• Labour		Staff Expenses	
• Materials		Subscription	
• Sub Trades		Tools	
• Preliminary & General		Travel costs	
TOTAL COGS	**$ 4,000,000**	Uncategorised Expense	
GROSS PROFIT	**$ 1,000,000**	Uniforms/Clothing	
		Utilities - Internet	
		Utilities - Mobile Phone	
		Wage Employees	
		Director Salaries	
		TOTAL EXPENSES	**$ 400,000**
		NET PROFIT	**$ 600,000**

$$\frac{1,000,000}{5,000,000} = 0.2$$
$$0.2 \times 100 = \mathbf{20\%}$$

$$\frac{400,000}{5,000,000} = 0.08$$
$$0.08 \times 100 = \mathbf{8\%}$$

$$\frac{600,000}{5,000,000} = 0.12$$
$$0.12 \times 100 = \mathbf{12\%}$$

The best way to do this is to review your Gross Profit, Expenses, and Net Profit in relation to total sales and view it as a percentage.

You can calculate these by taking the gross profit, expenses, and net profit figures and dividing each of them by the total sales figure. Then multiply by 100 to view the result as a percentage.

As a guideline, residential builders should expect to see ranges of 20%-25% gross profits, 8%-12% expenses (including your market rate salary as the business owner, fulfilling that role), and 10%-15% net profit.

We call these the Golden Ratios.

This leads me to the next step and a CRITICAL distinction.

YOUR MARKUP IS NOT YOUR MARGIN

A common pitfall over 93% of builders find themselves in is confusing markup with margin. This mistake will cost you hundreds of thousands of dollars. When you're pricing a job, are you simply putting, say, 10%, 15%, or 20% on it and considering that your profit margin?

Well, it's not. Here's why.

Above, we calculated margins. We took the gross profit and divided it by the sale price. This is the biggest difference between markup and margin.

Margin is the gross profit in relation to the sale price "cost to the client" whereas markup is the gross profit in relation to the "costs to you" or the cost of sale.

This could be why you might not have as much cash flow, profit, and money in the bank as you thought you should have.

Using the same numbers as above, and taking the "costs to you," for a job, then "whacking 20% on it", you are marking it up by 20%. But this 20% markup is actually only a 16.6% margin.

Let me explain.

20% of 16 Kiwi Way, a job costing you, $720,000 is $144,000. If we apply the 20% markup of $144,000 to $720,000, we end up with a *"cost to the client"* of $864,000. But $144,000 as a percentage of the sale price, or *"cost to the client"* of $864,000 is only 16.6% and not 20%. So while we thought we had a 20% margin, we actually have only a 16.6% margin.

Instead, to achieve the 20% margin we identified in the earlier P&L example, you must apply a minimum of 25% mark-up to the "cost to you" figures so that you achieve a 20% margin.

Use the table as a reference.

Mark Up Vs Margin Table The Ultimate Reference Check On Your Profits	
15% Mark up	13.0% Gross Profit Margin
20% Mark up	16.7% Gross Profit Margin
25% Mark up	20.0% Gross Profit Margin
30% Mark up	23.0% Gross Profit Margin
33.3% Mark up	25.0% Gross Profit Margin
43% Mark up	30.0% Gross Profit Margin
50% Mark up	33.0% Gross Profit Margin
75% Mark up	42.9% Gross Profit Margin
100% Mark up	50.0% Gross Profit Margin

If you are making the mistake of putting 10%, 15%, or 20% on your price and thinking it's your margin when it's in fact your markup, you're doing yourself a disservice and playing business with less cash flow to pay for operations and day-to-day business costs.

> "Before I met TPB, I had no clue about my numbers. I would apply a 10% markup on all my projects. Looking back at my numbers, I realize I was working backward, but I thought I was doing the right thing at the time. Now, my Gross profit is sitting at 25%."
>
> —Hayden N, Waikanae

Ok, so now you have set your P&L report up correctly and you have calculated your margin (not markup). The next step is to figure out what targets you should be aiming for.

WHY 20% GROSS PROFIT MARGIN?

The number one most important indicator of how well your building company is progressing is your gross margin. Think of it as the performance metric for the business. A low margin means things aren't performing well (or you're donating your time, expertise, liability, and team. You've got a hobby rather than creating a profitable business).

A low margin can mean the following:

- Your sales and marketing don't generate many leads for you to choose from, and you are forced to take any job just to keep your team busy.

- Prospects aren't positioned as to why they should choose you over anyone else, so they end up deciding on price, instead of considering the five key concerns of timeline, budget, trustworthiness, quality, and communication.

- You're pricing to win the work, not to make money, or you don't have a pricing for profit process in place to ensure projects are priced correctly to a target gross margin. This includes project management fees, P&G, and an overhead recovery margin.

It could also mean

- Your labour is blowing out.

- Materials are being wasted.

- Sub trades are not being scheduled correctly or not handing over quality work, causing delays and recalls.

- Change orders are missed, underpriced, or given for free by your team because they don't know what's in or out of the plans

Low margin also mean that

- You cannot pay yourself BOTH an operating salary and a "business owner bonus."

- You can't invest in good processes and systems, people, and help.

- You're stressed and will likely make more money with less risk and liability working for someone else.

It's important to remember, from your margin, or gross profit, you pay both the overheads (cost to run the business, including your salary) AND net profit ("business owner bonus" *or* "take home").

A high margin means you have at least a few things going well. So, the higher the gross margin, the bigger the opportunity to:

- Invest in better systems

- Have great cash flow

- Pay your guys more

- Recruit better team members and market for superstars

- Have great site signage and uniforms

- A great professional look/image to your company

- More cash in the bank to weather downturns

- Pay yourself more and get the car, boat, motorcycle you want

- Provide a higher level of service and support for your clients

- More flexibility in your negotiation and pricing

- Expand your business and make a great impact in your community

- Sponsor local community projects or a sports team

- Take more time out if you want for family and vacations

So, why at least 20%?

Well, anything under that makes it significantly harder to run a business with the right people, processes, and predictability. This can lead to feeling like you're not building a business but instead operating a busy job with overheads and liability. It may feel like you are stuck on the builder's hamster wheel, working hard but not getting ahead.

It's hard to operate with enough cash flow to not feel like you're run-ning the gauntlet. It's very difficult to get a return on your investment of at least 10% to 15% net profit as the business owner who is also in charge of tax obligations, health and safety, guarantees and warranties, and employing people.

> "We set up a workflow to track our numbers accurately, and I found that most of the contracts we signed are at a 20% margin. But most importantly, I finally have time for a date night during the weekends. Thanks, Marti!"
>
> —Ben E, Wellington

So clearly, business is better at 20% gross profit minimum. But what profit do YOU need?

WHAT IS YOUR DESIRED PROFIT?

After 20 years, we've worked with members growing $1m to $125m building companies and everything in between. We aren't in the business of telling you what your building company should look like. Instead, we help you build YOUR ideal business.

It may be highly profitable and/or give you plenty of freedom. Perhaps you want to run it from another city, or maybe you want to systemise it for sale or franchise. You could prioritise doing one great custom architectural project at a time, or you could build for scale.

These are different machines, requiring varying time commitments *from* you, and that create different financial opportunities *for* you and your family. That's why you must start with the end in mind, and plan to win, so you know what business you're building.

PLAY TO WIN

Let's go through how to approach this together.

If you'd like to make $300,000 net profit in the next 12 months, work out what your fixed costs are. If your fixed costs are $200,000, add that to your desired outcome, and you get a total fixed cost of $500,000. This is the overall number to hit that ensures you get paid what you are worth and have enough money to expand the business and pay all your fixed costs.

Perhaps you want an office manager, pricing support or software, and a bigger marketing budget alongside a salary pay rise for you and your project manager. We can now reverse engineer the requirements for the business, by using the break even equation (or our 4 levers calculator).

$$\left(\text{BREAK EVEN} = \frac{\text{FIXED COSTS}}{\text{GP \%}} \right)$$

BREAK EVEN FORMULA

$$\$1.75M = \frac{\$350K}{0.2}$$

BREAK EVEN SAMPLE

So What Is Your Desired Profit?

GP Margin	Revenue	Ave $ Sale	
		$250k	$500k
10%	$ 5 M	20	10
15%	$ 3.75 M	15	7.5
20%	$ 2.5 M	10	5
25%	$ 2 M	8	4

* Your gross profit margin dictates the number of projects you need to do.

In this example, if you have a combined goal of $500,000 in gross profit (to pay for a $300,000 net profit and $200,000 in overheads) and a gross margin of only 10%. You have to do $5 million worth of projects. If you can get a higher gross margin of 15%, the amount of revenue required drops to $3.75 million. If you hit your ideal target margin of at least 20%, you now only have to do $2.5 million in total sales to cover all your overheads (fixed costs of $200,000) and make your net profit of $300,000.

If you had continued to confuse markup with margin and thought you had a 25% margin (whereas that 25% was actually your markup), you'd have to do $2.5 million in projects instead of the $2 million you'd actually have to do to make your desired profit. That's $500,000 less!

> *"I'm in control of my numbers. I've been using pricing for profit, quotes as an action plan, positioning yourself, and a strong belief in our systems, [which] has led to this moment. Just signed a contract for $750K with a 25% margin, and ALL of my contracts will be at this margin or more from now on."*
>
> —Brian M, Dunedin

You can then identify the break-even amount by removing the target net profit figure of $300,000 and just calculating based on overheads of $200,000 divided by your gross margin of 20%.

This shows you need to complete total sales of $1m to break even.

> *"When I started, I didn't know what a target gross margin was. I would price a job and have no clue what the margin was. I thought I was winning. I didn't know how to run a profitable business. TPB helped me understand the numbers I needed to aim for."*
>
> —Mark T, Tauranga

ENSURE YOU HIT (OR SURPASS) THE GOLDEN RATIOS

Gross Profit	20% +
Overheads (including Owners Salary)	8% - 12%
Net Profit	10% +

NOW WHAT?

The action plan for you for this chapter is to get your numbers dialed in. Use the **4 Levers Profit Calculator** to achieve this.

4 Levers Profit Calculator

	Per Quarter (Now)	Per Quarter (in 90 Days)
Leads	8	12
Conversion Rate	25%	33%
Jobs	2	4
Average Sale Value	$ 250,000	$ 300,000
Quarterly Revenue	$ 500,000	$ 1,188,000
Yearly Revenue	$ 2,000,000	$ 4,752,000
Gross Profit Margin %	15%	20%
Total Gross Profit	$ 300,000	$ 950,400
Fixed Costs	$ 150,000	$ 320,000
NET PROFIT	**$ 150,000**	**$ 630,400**

Plan out which of these areas has the most opportunity that you are going to take action on in the next 90 days, and then start setting some targets. If you just put three strategies into place over the next 90 days to improve the number that has the biggest opportunity, you can make massive gains in both profit and cash flow.

ACTION STEPS

Business is a numbers game. They tell a story of what's working well in your business and where to focus for the biggest impact.

1. Make sure you get an accurate Profit and Loss, and Key Performance Indicator report each month. Compare this with your budget.

2. Price to your desired target margin, which should be what works best for your business niche—ideally 20%-25% gross profit margin.

3. Plug your numbers into the *4 Financial Levers Calculator* to see what's possible for your business 12 months from now—with the right strategies.

Scan the code for all the resources:

KNOW THE NUMBERS THAT DRIVE YOUR BUSINESS

Here are a few of our members' results:

★★★★★

I finished a course with TPB and must admit it has been the single most beneficial business decision I have made.

In November I felt like I had no life or direction. Now I have time, direction, systems in place and my hunger is back.

Last year I was a builder and now I feel like a Business owner/operator.

Thank TPB Crew. If you're on the fence, get off and do it.

Matt B
Australia

★★★★★

We had a lot of projects in the pipeline but had no systems to help keep things on track and also keep profits in the company. We highly recommend TPB, as **they have helped us make strides toward increasing profits** and building much more efficient processes.

Richard L
California, USA

★★★★★

TPB has been instrumental on helping me increase my profit margins and run my business more efficiently. I discovered areas where I was losing money that I wasn't aware of. I've also got better team morale and relationships with my sub contractors from some of the things I've learned. The instruction and coaching is top notch, and if you are in the building trades and want to improve your game, I strongly recommend using their service to help you do it!

Shandra C
Texas, USA

★★★★★

Before engaging with TPB I was running a business with **no systems, poor cash flow and no pipeline of work**.
Working with TPB has changed my business and also changed my life.
After putting in the work that is guided by such a great team of coaches I have now gained back time with my family which was most important to me.
Not only time with my family was gained but my profit has now tripled in the duration of 13 months in the most toughest times with Lockdowns and my pipeline of work is booked for the next 18 months!
Huge thank you to the team at TPB for not only guiding me in creating a great business but giving me the tools to get my time back with my family.

I will continue to work in with this team when needed as they made such a massive change in myself as a business owner.

Mark T
Tauranga, NZ

USING THESE NUMBERS TO BECOME PROFITABLE

Now that you understand your numbers, the next thing to focus on is how to get paid what you're worth, which we'll cover in the next chapter. Once you understand what should go into your price, you can set a minimum gross margin that will allow you to achieve your profit objectives. We'll also cover renovations specifically, and how to control the job so your expenses don't get out of hand and you preserve the relationship with your client.

MEMBER PROFILE: LUKE S.

When I first met Luke, the only number he knew was his revenue. He didn't know what his profit margins were and didn't back cost his jobs. All he did was put a markup on his projects and thought he would make a good profit by the end of the project.

But when he met his bookkeeper to run the numbers, he had barely made any profit. Sometimes he was even losing money on jobs. This wasn't what Luke had in mind when he started his building business.

He was about to close up shop and go work for someone else. He would earn the same amount without having to deal with cash flow issues, health and safety risks, worrying about his business 24/7, and sacrificing his time with the family.

Luke has always been driven and hard-working, but he lacked clarity about his numbers.

Know and Show Your Numbers

To fix this, we helped him work out his current numbers and gave him clarity on the minimum margins he needed to aim for. We updated his old pricing structure and worked with him to hone his sales process, which allowed him to charge higher prices with less price resistance and to be paid what he is worth for the great quality work he does. After a few months, his sales inquiries steadily increased, and he constantly quoted new jobs with the pricing for profit method.

By understanding his numbers, Luke course-corrected and made the right decision based on his profit and loss statement. He knows how to control his work in progress and keep his overhead costs low throughout the project. It saved his business and allowed him to experience how it feels to run a profitable business rather than just a busy job with overheads.

Today, he's on track to make $2.5m in turnover with a 15% net profit. He plans to grow his wealth by diving into investment and property development.

CHAPTER 5 – SUMMARY
PRICE YOUR PROJECTS PROFITABLY

- Pricing is your biggest tool for profit improvement.

- Price to your target gross margin. That allows you to cover your overheads and hit your net profit goals.

- Ensure you get paid for your time and include Project Management Fees and Overhead Recovery Margin

- Capture and invoice variations weekly to improve cashflow and so there are no nasty surprises for the client at the end of the project.

- Report your labour hours by stage to your team to let them know if they are on track and what to do if they are off track (in the toolbox meeting).

- Aim to get your actual labour hours to within 5% of forecast by stage.

- Control WIP by reporting your numbers with your team each week and incentivise them to hit the targets.

PRICE YOUR PROJECTS PROFITABLY

*Pricing is by far the biggest
tool for earnings improvement.*
–McKinsey & Co

Pricing means knowing and understanding what a project is worth. It means setting a minimum target gross margin overall—not just putting dollars per hour onto your guys and whacking 5%, 10%, or 15% onto materials. Upon calculating the costs of doing the job, the profitable builder would set at least a 20% gross margin over the whole project.

If you had a job that was an $800,000 cost to you in labour, materials, and subcontractors. You would price the job at least $1 million dollars to the client. This price will meet all of your projected profit and expenses—as long as you control the labour, materials, and sub-contractors throughout the job.

FROM INQUIRY TO PRICING A JOB

Upon showing the client your concept design, do a quick price estimate. This immediately lets the client know that the design they have chosen is within their ballpark.

In the process of creating a high-level estimate, it's crucial to have a database that enables you to provide the client with an immediate quote. This database should include your default settings, such as material prices, supplier information, and basic take-off data. If a merchant sends you a file, you can simply upload it to the database.

For example, roofing generally costs around $65 NZD per square metre, and windows are approximately $400 per square metre. Use these standard rates for initial estimates to give the client an early sense of their budget.

It's important to note that these estimates are based on standard square metre (m²) or linear metre (l/m) rates for general construction costs. As the client finalizes their plans and selects specifications, you'll need to review their schedule, obtain detailed quotes from suppliers, and assess standard rates from merchants for accurate pricing.

Add up all the costs, and for labour, apply a formula that reflects the specific tasks expected. This could include activities such as flooring, sanding frames, or working with purlins. By customising your labour estimates according to these factors, you can ensure a more accurate and reliable cost projection.

At this stage, it's crucial to refer to up-to-date and accurate resources for estimating project durations and costs. Rather than relying on outdated construction handbooks, consider using current pricing software such as Buildaprice or Buildxact, or build your own spreadsheet, which offer more accurate and real-world data. These tools will help you adjust your estimates based on the complexity of the project and the specific roles of your team members.

This is an example of one of our members' pricing spreadsheets:

For larger views of the tables featured in this book, scan the QR code at the end of each chapter to access a complete list of resources and images.

Stage	Stage Allowance	Stage Costs	Raw P/L
Demolition	$ 31,161.06	-	$ 31,161.06
Site establishment	$ 24,339.25	-	$ 24,339.25
Foundation and Floors	$ 49,890.98	$ 5,015.00	$ 44,875.98
Framing and Trusses	$ 75,337.34	-	$ 75,337.34
Roof and Fascia	$ 37,251.30	-	$ 37,251.30
Windows and Cladding	$ 96,026.37	-	$ 96,026.37
Preline	$ 56,581.66	-	$ 56,581.66
Linings, stopping, Painting	$ 59,268.23	-	$ 59,268.23
Completion	$ 91,620.26	-	$ 91,620.26
Landscaping	$ 35,750.00	$ 37,378.46	$ 1,628.46

Total	$ 557,226.45
Check Field from Totals sheet	$ 557,226.45

Stage	Total	O/H allowance	Margin	Total	GST Inclusive	Labour Allowances	
						Demo	$ 6,161.06
Site Establishment	$ 24,339.25	$ 2,818.02	$ 3,056.80	$ 30,214.07	$ 34,746.18	Found and Floors	$ 7,133.63
Demolition	$ 31,161.06	$ 3,607.85	$ 3,913.56	$ 38,682.48	$ 44,484.85	Framing	$ 15,972.04
Foundation and Floors	$ 49,890.98	$ 5,776.42	$ 6,265.87	$ 61,933.27	$ 71,223.26	Roof	$ 2,164.43
Framing and Trusses	$ 75,337.34	$ 8,722.62	$ 9,461.72	$ 93,521.67	$ 107,549.92	Windows	$ 11,105.71
Roof and Fascia	$ 37,251.30	$ 4,312.99	$ 4,678.44	$ 46,242.72	$ 53,179.13	Preline	$ 2,258.97
Windows and Cladding	$ 96,026.37	$ 11,118.02	$ 12,060.08	$ 119,204.47	$ 137,085.14	Lings to paint	$ 3,788.85
Preline	$ 56,581.66	$ 6,551.07	$ 7,106.17	$ 70,238.90	$ 80,774.74	completion	$ 4,510.33
Linings, stopping, Painting	$ 59,268.23	$ 6,862.13	$ 7,443.58	$ 73,573.93	$ 84,610.02	Landscaping	$ 540.00
Completion	$ 91,620.26	$ 10,607.87	$ 11,506.71	$ 113,734.84	$ 130,795.07		
Landscaping	$ 35,750.00	$ 4,139.17	$ 4,489.89	$ 44,379.06	$ 51,035.91	Total	$ 53,635.02
Overhead Allowance	$ 64,516.16						
Margin	$ 69,982.81						
Referal fee	$ 6,917.25			$ 6,917.25	$ 7,954.84		
Total	$ 698,642.67	$ 64,516.16	$ 69,982.81	$ 698,642.67			
Gst	$ 104,796.40	$ 9,677.42	$ 10,497.42	$ 104,796.40			
Grand Total	$ 803,439.07	$ 74,193.58	$ 80,480.23	$ 803,439.07	$ 803,439.07		

Now, let's say you have estimated that the roof's going to cost you $50,000. If the roof quote comes in and it's close, you know your estimation process is effective.

But if the roof price comes in and it's, say, $75,000, ask the roofer why it's so expensive. He may say there are more valleys and hips in there than you thought there were. Or he might say, "Dimonds[1] just put up their materials by 30%", in which case you go and adjust your square metre rate for the estimate stage.

---

[1] A roofing manufacturer in New Zealand.

BUILDER'S ROADMAP TIP:

DOUBLE-CHECK YOUR INVOICES.

When you receive an invoice from a subcontractor, have your office manager check it against the purchase order to see if it's correct. If it's wrong, go back to the supplier that day and say, "What's going on here?" Some of our members have avoided paying between $2,000 and $15,000 per job in invoicing errors because they included this step in their pricing process.

Something else that could occur is, say, the electrician halfway through the month charges a progress payment[2], but he actually managed to finish the job by the end of the month. Then he bills you at the end of the month for the whole amount of work. So, you have two invoices there. One for half the amount and another one for the full amount. So if you paid him without looking at what you're paying for, you would be paying him the cost of the job plus extra.

This gives you a pretty good guide to start and perhaps even allows you to get to your estimate level done in under an hour. But to establish a proper price, you've got to go through the plans page by page, detail by detail, and fine-tune the quantities and what suppliers you'll use. This way, you can establish what you need quotes for and where from. It normally takes a good day or two to get all of this accurate.

For example, to price a $300,000 new build, the estimate stage would take about half an hour, but there would probably be another seven or eight hours to get the price as accurate as you can.

The following are the steps for thorough pricing of a project.

---

[2] Payments made based on costs incurred by the subcontractor.

PRICING PROJECTS ACCURATELY AND QUICKLY

Step 1: First off, get the plans.

You cannot accurately price a sketch or an incomplete set of drawings. Make sure you have access to a complete set of plans or can work with the client and their team (or your team) to create an accurate set.

Step 2: Second, get the materials and add your markup.

Let's say all the materials came to a $400,000 cost to your company. With a 25% markup on those materials, you add $100,000 to that cost. (And remember: markup is not your margin!) That's really simple on a fixed-price contract.

Step 3: Once the materials are in, look at your margins.[3]

During this stage, look at what you've allocated towards overheads, including:

- Sales costs
- Administration costs
- Project management costs
- Travel[4]
- Health and safety
- Allowance for inspecting the site and taking levels
- Engineer's fees
- Temporary power

---

[3] Overhead costs are about nine to 10% of the job, per job, if you spread it out across the whole year. A lot of people don't actually understand the impact that the overheads have on their pricing. And obviously you have to pay that before you start making any profit. So, if you're not getting that as part of your price on the project, then you're going backwards on each job.

[4] If a project is out of town, use your standard town rates. And before you get quotes in, estimate using previous jobs that the cost will go up a bit based on travel costs; this number can be $5,000 depending on distance. For instance, your concrete deliveries might be a little bit out of town, and you've got to factor in those delivery costs too. And when you've fine-tuned that price, that travel cost can disappear from your invoices and be allocated to other costs.

- Design costs[5]

- Colour consultation

- Master Build guarantee fees and membership fees

- Builders' risk insurance

- Allowance for a bit of contingency

- Gifts for the client

- Welcome pack

- Professional clean of the client's home.

It's best to add as many allowances as you can for extra overheads. Try to include your office overheads on a per-job basis. For example, you can add about $600 to the price of each job for your accounting fees, $500 on each job for potential lawyer fees, and include items like the disposal of trash and the rental of portaloos.[6] All these costs you should put in your preliminary stage. Once you've got all those costs in, get them narrowed down so there are no surprises.

BUILDER'S ROADMAP TIP:

AIM ABOVE YOUR OVERHEADS.

Aim to have a net profit margin of between 10% and 15% after overheads are paid. Then aim for a 20%-25% gross profit margin for the whole project.

It may seem a lot, but honestly, you've got to do that. If you're pricing your margins low, you end up doing a lot of work, you get busy, you can't afford to get the extra people on to help you and you're running around like crazy. Then at the end of the day, you find you've made no money, and you would've been better off going fishing or getting a job and working for someone else.

---

[5] When it comes to LIM reports and PIM reports, the client doesn't supply these nor is it a cost you eat. You take that out of your design costs. Before you start designing is when you acquire them. And since you'll also spend quite a bit of time on the site digging holes, finding the pegs and taking levels, consider this process part of design costs as well.

[6] Another word for portable toilets.

Step 4: The next step is to forecast the labour.

The rule of thumb is to cost your margin into the labour rate you're charging for each individual hour of labour. Work out a charge-out rate for each builder before you start. For example, an apprentice may be charging out at $45, but you may be passing on $25 of that to them.

A WORD ON PROJECT MANAGEMENT FEES

Are you charging a project management fee? If you're not, you absolutely should. Building projects require hours upon hours of project management, and without this role, the project simply isn't possible. This qualifies it as a fixed cost (or can be a variable cost if billed per project to each client).

Avoid lumping the project management fee with other items like tarpaulins and portaloos. Instead, it's more effective to keep the project management fee separate from these costs. This transparency helps prevent any concerns about billing rates, as the fee is clearly outlined rather than embedded in overall costs.

For smaller jobs, you might consider incorporating project manage-ment costs into your hourly rate. Typically, project management fees can range from 3% to 6% of the total project cost.

On some of the bigger jobs, it could just be a set figure. If you've got a project manager who you're paying $100,000 per year and you've got a job that's going for three months, you might take a quarter of their salary and apply that to the total project management fee for the job plus your desired markup of 25% to get your 20% gross profit margin.

The good thing is that now project management fees are widely accepted. It used to be really hard to charge a project management fee, but everyone now expects one. You can't sit there and question your builder on how many hours you took for the job if every day you spent two hours running to the council, ordering materials and subcon-tractors, and talking to the client—that's all project management.

NAVIGATING THE CLIENT-FACING ASPECT OF PRICING

Many builders starting out use charge-up contracts, where clients pay for each item as it's invoiced, providing transparency throughout the project. This method is often seen as lower risk due to its clear, itemized billing.

However, it's important to consider the potential disadvantages. Charge-up contracts require additional administration time, as you need to manage and document each item carefully. This approach also demands more accurate bookkeeping and back costing to ensure all costs are accounted for and to avoid discrepancies.

On the other hand, the client will see all the items, so they'll generally tend to ask more questions, and there's more administration with that. You've really got to be on top of your game throughout the whole build if this happens.

> *"Thanks to Marti and TPB, I have more confidence to charge more and focus on that 20%+ gross profit. One client told me that price is not a huge factor as we have come across as the most professional builders that they have approached, and they really want to use our service."*
>
> –Josh B, Wellington

More experienced builders, on the other hand, tend to go with fixed-price contracts in which they could tag out[7] certain elements of the project. The positive aspect of the fixed-price contract from the client's point of view is that they know exactly where they stand.

One downside to fixed-price contracts is that if you get it wrong—if you don't account for everything—you're losing money and time and can risk

---

[7] To tag something out means to exclude a particular item from the fixed price quote because it's something you might be unsure about and can't guarantee a specific price or time frame for before the job starts.

the rapport between you and the client. The key to doing fixed prices correctly is to back cost as the job goes. You need to know every dollar being spent every day of the job and, if there is an issue, be in a position to address it quickly.

There have been many instances in which builders have not accounted for changes in the terms of a contract. A client might say to a carpenter on site, "Hey, can you just move that doorway?" and the carpenter—not thinking of the implications—just goes ahead and does it, but they don't get it priced first or signed off. These situations often leave the building company owner wondering where all the labour hours went.

Let the client know what you're doing before you start. If there is a change, price it out and get them to sign off a contract variation[8] straight away—before it proceeds—so they know the impact of the change and there's no argument later. Doing this takes the financial pressure out of the equation. Have a pre-construction meeting and let the client know that there are to be no changes unless it's through the office and priced and signed off.

THE IMPORTANCE OF SIGNING OFF ON CONTRACT VARIATIONS

It happens to the best of us. One of our members who has won the Registered Master Builders' House of the Year Award had an experience where he was building a house for a client, and one of the client's buddies was getting his house built by our member's building company at the same time.

As time went on, the friend got more and more ideas as he compared his job to that of his friend, so he kept asking the building company to make this change, add that, etc. The friend assumed the building company would simply accommodate anything, but at the end of the job, he had racked up an extra $40,000 he didn't expect. Situations like these cause

---

[8] This refers to a variation in a contract, the part of the contract that will change from its original terms based on an agreement between both parties while the rest of the contract's terms stay the same.

unnecessary conflict between the builder and the client that could have been avoided with upfront communication. This is where variations/change orders come in.

There are three scenarios in which to do a variation:

1. **If the client asks for a change.** This one is a simple process of filling out a variation order, pricing it, and letting the client know the difference. They sign it off before you go ahead.

2. When you order materials and **the client asks for something different on site from what you've allowed for.** If this happens, ask why it's different, and let them know that it might generate a variation.

3. When you get an **invoice from a subcontractor or a supplier and it's different to what you ordered** or different to what he quoted. If this happens, tell the subcontractor or supplier that you'll try and recover the difference in price from the client. If you can't, it's the subcontractor/supplier's cost. You only have to do that once or twice, and it gets rid of the problem—it's on them at that point.

In your purchase orders, it's good to include the phrase, "No variations unless approved by the office first," so it's pretty clear.

> *"We are constantly quoting and pricing jobs correctly, maintaining a clear timeframe for the subcontractors and our guys on site. All this with that 15% net profit in mind. I wouldn't be at this stage without the help from TPB."*
>
> –Luke S, Illawarra

The problem with the first-time buyer is that they've typically got a limited budget. All of a sudden, they might get some money and want to change things. If this happens, you'll want to say to them, "Look, when you signed this contract, we gave you this price based on you keeping things simple. It's your first home. Please don't overcomplicate it for yourself or us, or it's just going to drag on and get too expensive." Building the house with the materials on charge-up will alleviate the problem. Have your QS do a good takeoff at the start and put a clause into the contract stating what you *expect* materials to cost, but you ultimately need to charge the client based on the actual cost.

In your contracts, it's important to be clear on not just what's included but also on what's excluded. This will prevent issues for you later.

Now Let's Talk About the Job Itself

All of this upfront pricing comes from the experience of doing jobs regularly and making sure you're accounting for everything that could go wrong or go over in terms of time and money. There's also the profit you're factoring in to make sure you're making money on the job from the start.

There are a myriad of things you can do *on-site* as well to make sure you're within your estimates and timelines. You need to make sure you're making money on the job all the way through while it's happening in real time and definitely not losing any money. This ties into how you communicate with your team, structure their work, communicate your expectations of them, and make sure their labour hours match the forecast hours you did for their role in the build. The next section will close out the chapter with tips on how to control the job while it's happening to minimise surprises and achieve a systemised process and orderly project.

> *"I'm using TPB's checklist in all of my processes. We use the 287 Point Quality Control Checklist, pre-walkthrough, and post-walkthrough. We saved so much time with these checklists. We usually took 2 months to wrap up a project, but with these checklists, it only took 2 weeks."*
>
> —Ben C, British Columbia

CONTROLLING THE JOB ON SITE TO STAY ON TRACK

Before you actually start a job, your foreman should have a set of plans and a job folder with detailed information, which he has a good look through. Your foreman might spend a couple of days actually understanding the work outlined by the plan and which subcontractor is doing what. If you're doing a $1 million project, spending a day or two preparing for that job is actually money saved. The foreman has to be intimate with the job and know the scope of work (what's included and not included) and what qualifies as a variation. One of the key things for him to know is what the exclusions are—what's not included. It should be very clear in your contracts what all of these are going to be.

Once the job is running, you need to make sure each facet of the job is being covered. Grab screenshots or pictures of how to perform the tasks expected of your team. *Show* people what they need to do rather than just being a talking head. You might have a screenshot of the 287-point quality assurance checklist for your foreman to use.

QUALITY CONTROL

Date:	Project:	Completed by:

B		Set out and Foundation	Pass	Fail	N/A	Date
Tasks	1	Boundaries have been identified by surveyor and datum established				
	2	Profiles have been installed, minimum 2m away from building line				
	3	Set out checked and within a 2mm tolerance over 20m				
	4	Footings/piles excavation on solid ground. If in doubt engineer contacted				
	5	Reinforcing steel installed as per plans engineer details take presidency				
	6	Concrete cover to reinforcing to meet engineers' specs.				
	7	Heights for footing checked against datum, height pegs within 2mm				
	8	Position of all started rods checked and aligned for block work and engineer specs.				
	9	Timber piles-ensure treated and installed to bottom and correct treatment				
	10	Concrete punch pads installed for piles where required				
Health and Safety	11	Barriers installed, public safety ensured				
	12	Exposed excavation batters have polythene protection from erosion				
	13	Excavation of trench deeper than 1.5m has hordings installed				
	14	HI VIZ is being worn around machinery				
	15	Reinforcing safety caps installed				
	16	Roads and access are kept clean Wash down station set up if required				
	17	No silt run off to go into any drainage Refer to council's provision if required				
	18	Concrete wash down area determined Ensure NO contamination of drainage				
	19	All tools and machinery are used correctly and safely				

BUILDER'S ROADMAP TIP:

PREP YOUR TEAM MEMBERS ON WHAT'S TO COME FOR THE FOLLOWING WORK DAY.

One important thing you want to do with anyone on your team (especially young apprentices) is to let them know what they're doing the next day. So, rather than springing it on them at 7:00 a.m., they already know in advance and can mentally and physically prepare for what's to come during the week.

Break it down by stage to show your team exactly what they are each expected to do. Then, come back through and get the foreman to run you through the quality assurance checklist. As the business owner, if you see something that's not up to par, you can say, "Hey, that's not good enough. Here's what we want." Then, once you're comfortable and he's confident, he can follow the checklist and you can manage the jobs without having to be there all the time.

> "After joining TPB, I had my longest holiday in the last 11 years! I went from being a control freak to delegating my tasks. There are systems in place for the office and on site, so I don't have to worry when I'm away."
>
> —Wade H, Melbourne

THE RULES OF THE GAME

What I'm about to show you next is something that seems elementary but is often overlooked. You've got to give your team members what the rules of the game are for each build and have them sign a sheet saying they will comply. Otherwise, how will they know how the build is supposed to go? And how will you know they will do the things you ask of them? The Rules of the Game sheet, given by the foreman to the rest of the team for a certain building project, could include things like:

1. "We will wear our uniforms."

2. "We will have our time sheets in on time."

3. "We won't drop nails in the driveway."

4. "We only have one radio on site. You can take turns every other day, change channels, but only use one radio."

5. "No dogs on the site."

BUILDER'S ROADMAP TIP:

CONTROL HOW MATERIALS ARE HANDLED WITH YOUR RULES OF THE GAME.

Make sure the guys measure twice and cut once and that they know you're trying to save some money, not trying to just cut willy-nilly. This can be enforced in your Rules of the Game. Also, have the foreman and project manager check the jumbo bins each week.

Any new person that joins your company, as part of their employment contract, should also sign the Rules of the Game. It's really good to be able to go back if there's an issue. Here's an example of one of our members' Rules of the Game:

Rules of the Game

Looking after each other:

We are all part of a team. Respect each other. Help each other. Communicate well. If someone seems to be having a down day, check if they are ok. Work as a team. Laugh with, not at.

Enjoyment:

Have fun at work. Be passionate about what you do. Be positive. If you are feeling down, talk about it.

Conduct:

Think about the image you are portraying. Be courteous and kind to all visitors on site. Is the language you are using appropriate for the person you are talking too?

Mistakes:

We all make them. Own up. Don't try to hide it. Learn from it. Move on!

Hours of work:

Hours of work vary, depending on job timeframes, location, etc. but are generally between 8.00am - 5.00pm, Monday - Friday

If you need to leave your job early for any reason (i.e. to go to the dentist, doctor, bank, etc.) inform your foreman at least the day before. If planning to be off work for a whole day please give us one week notice in advance.

Time sheets:

Time sheets are to be filled in daily to help keep it accurate.

For jobs in Christchurch your time starts when you get to site, unless you need to pick up materials on the way, and then start your time from when you leave home. For jobs out of Christchurch your time starts when you leave home - record as 'travel time' in Flexitime.

You are entitled to 30 minutes of paid break per day. Record any break time over 30 minutes in your time sheet. E.g. If you have a total of 1 hour of breaks, record 30 minutes in your time sheet. If you have a total of 1 hour and 15 minute break, record 45 minute in your time sheet. If you are going to the shop during your break, the time taken to go to the shop is included as break time.

Start and finishing times need to be accurate. Make sure times are accurate when moving from job to job. Any discrepancy in time sheets will be seen as misconduct.

Health and Safety:

You are responsible for your own safety and the safety of those around you. Inform visitors to site of the hazards and ensure they sign in. Follow health and safety procedures. Continually check for new hazards. Warn others. Watch each other's backs. Don't assume they know. No one is exempted from Health and Safety requirements. If it's not safe, or you don't feel comfortable, don't do it.

Smoking:

No smoking during working time. If smoking during your break please smoke outside away from non smokers. Dispose of butts safely and cleanly.

Uniform:

Work uniform needs to be worn at all times. Uniforms must be washed regular and kept in good condition. If doing something really messy (i.e. painting), remove your work jacket/hoodie first or wear overalls.

Phones:

Make sure your mobile phone is charged and you have enough credit to be able to text your supervisor if you need to. Limit personal phone calls during working hours. Don't use client's landline unless you ask the client first. Work related only of course.

Site Tidiness:

At the end of the day clean your work site. This includes your lunch rubbish. When working on renovations or nearly completed new builds always use drop sheets to protect floor coverings.

Materials:

All materials should be organised in advance by the Site Foreman. When ordering or purchasing materials you must use an order reference which is the jobs full street address. (i.e. 9 Coronation St, not just Coronation St).

When taking delivery of materials ensure you check off what has been delivered. Check picking slip vs what has been delivered and what has been ordered. Report any anomalies to your foreman. Check delivered items for damage and report any damage immediately.

Tools:

Respect all tools. If using another person's personal tools, ask their permission first. Any broken tools need to be reported and handed into Site Foreman and not used as this will cause more damage. If wanting to purchase your own tools on our account you must ask the account owner first.

Drugs/Alcohol:

No alcohol/drug use during work time. If you have had a hard night and aren't fit to work then don't come. Working under the influence of drugs or alcohol may result in instant dismissal.

Vehicles:

Respect company vehicles and report any damage immediately. You must pay for any fines you get while using a company vehicle.

Problems:

If you have a problem, talk to us so we can sort it out. We can't help if we don't know about it.

Extras...

_____

_____

_____

_____

GETTING YOUR FORECAST LABOUR HOURS RIGHT

One of the biggest aspects of controlling the job on site is to make sure labour hours stay within your forecast. This is why it's so crucial to focus on getting your forecast as close as possible to your actual labour hours with each job *before* it starts.

This is where most jobs blow out. One of the great tools you can use is to start tracking your labour hours each and every day and compare your forecast versus the actual. This way, it's not just one big batch of 2,000 hours; it's 10-18 stages broken down by how long each stage will take. And you can let your team know daily/weekly whether they are on track or not.

"Hey, we are at 65 hours for the framing out of the 100 allocated, and we're not halfway through."

The foreman can then say to the guys on site, "We're 15 hours over budget. What can we do to pull back those 15 hours? Otherwise, no one is getting their bonus." Controlling the job in real time will massively increase your productivity, profitability, and accuracy in quoting future jobs. You should be aiming to get within 5% of the forecast labour hours by stage and refine this as you go.

To ultimately enforce the outcome you wish to occur, such as your team putting in the hours that are needed or doing the job faster in less time, one method is to offer incentives. Here's an approach you can try:

1. Involve the foreman in planning the project and calculating labour hours by stage.

2. Have the foreman go in-depth through the plans, scope of work, and contract and know what's an inclusion or exclusion and what constitutes a variation.

3. Have a pre-construction meeting with all subcontractors.

4. Clear timelines and project management.

5. Know and show the labour hours by stage with your team.

6. Have weekly toolbox meetings to update the team.

7. Back cost in real time.

8. Control your Work In Progress.

9. Have weekly construction meetings.

10. Incentivise your foreman/supervisor and your crew based on productivity, quality, and communication.

PROFITABLE BUILDERS INCENTIVISE PRODUCTIVITY

The company wins by doing the job under budget and under time with great quality. Therefore, you've got to incentivise your team to prioritise this. One way to incentivise your team could be to give each of them between $100 and $250 over a 10-week job if it is done within time and under budget. A simple way to measure their success is to use the daily site logs.

Get the guys to fill in what they did stage by stage. This means logging how long it took to put the slab down or get the framing done. It means being as specific as writing down that they thought it was going to be 80 hours total to get the framing up, but it took 75 hours instead, or that they thought interior linings were going to be 100 hours, but they actually took 123. This way, you, as the business owner, can figure out why it took longer than it should have. Maybe it's because John and Bob are good friends and they talk too much—which means you shouldn't have John and Bob working together.

Or maybe Bob needs more training. Maybe John's a grumpy foreman, and Bob's a hammerhand or an apprentice, so he's too scared to ask John any questions. In a situation like this, you can just have a chat with John and say, "Hey, did you realise you're being a bit of a grumpy bugger? It's actually leading to a lot of remedial work."

This way, everything's filled in every day. It doesn't take much to fill in a form and you get so much value out of it. It's worth giving your employees the time to do this. You can use the Buildertrend app on-site for the guys to fill in the information as they go on site.

BUILDER'S ROADMAP TIP:

GIVE BONUSES FOR EXTRA WORK HOURS PUT IN BY YOUR WORKERS.

In your Rules of the Game, I suggest you include a weekly bonus of about $60 for each employee who puts in 4 extra (productive) hours at work[9] (be sure to define and communicate exactly what is expected of them during those extra hours) to keep everyone motivated. That bonus is how your team wins. If you've got 10 guys you pay $60 each that week, it will cost you $600, but those extra 40 hours of work by all 10 guys brought back $2,400 in total per week. So, if you multiply your gross profit of $1,800 by the 50 weeks you work in the year, you get an extra $90,000 gross profit. The extra profit made from your team members winning is how the company wins.

TO CONCLUDE: RESPECT THE PROCESS OF PRICING PROJECTS

The biggest thing is to take your time. A lot of clients now think it's similar to walking onto a car lot where you've got the price displayed in the window, and they can't understand why building a house takes a while to price.

It's a matter of educating clients that it does take time to get them the best price and negotiate with the subcontractors and suppliers properly.

Another biggie is you've got to have those margins in there. It's really easy to miss stuff, and you can't get every job perfect. There have been jobs where builders missed all the doors, for example, and that took a bit of catching up. But you only do that once.

[9] You don't have to work Saturdays and neither does your crew, unless you really need to push a specific project.

If I were to leave you with just one thing, I'd say that the biggest opportunity is the back costing in real time; spending just 15 minutes a day on this will prevent a lot of issues. You can't just cost a job and not back cost it. You've got to be on your back costing every day because that's where you can see what's not right and you can modify it very quickly. Yes, back costing is hard work, but it's this kind of discipline that really makes a big difference to the bottom line.

I know everyone hates pricing. It's one of those things that when you're doing it, you feel like you're not being productive, but if you don't get that right, everything else you're doing is really a waste of time.

If you follow these steps, you will improve your gross margin, the number one indicator of how well your building company is doing. So, make sure you go through the pricing steps and tick those processes off. Observe all the tips in this chapter. Again, start with what area in your pricing is the most painful or the biggest area of frustration and start making changes there. Make sure that you are getting paid what you are worth for your time.

ACTION STEPS

1. Price to a minimum target gross margin of 20%-25%, including project management fees and overhead recovery margin.

2. Back cost in real time to control your Work In Progress and keep on top of your labour hours by stage vs. forecast hours.

3. Invoice your variations weekly and get them signed off to improve cash flow and avoid any nasty client surprises at the end of the project.

Scan the code for all the resources:

MEMBER PROFILE: DEAN W.

Dean specialises in residential renovations, additions, and landscaping.

From 1992 to 2015, Dean took three different shots at starting and scaling a successful building company, but each time he noticed a familiar pattern: feeling like he was on top of the world after landing a few jobs and then crashing back down when he checked the end balance. By 2019, he was doing $1.5M in revenue, but profits were slim.

Dean decided he wasn't just going to sit around and let history repeat itself. He started searching for a business coach but kept running into guys who had Harvard Business degrees but didn't really understand construction. He narrowed his search for a builders-specific training program and stumbled upon The Professional Builder website. After listening to the stories of other TPB members who had taken the leap of faith and gotten results, he jumped all in.

Execute Like a Man Possessed

Dean immediately started executing on everything his coaches gave him, and one of the first roadblocks he destroyed was feeling like he had to do everything himself. Like a lot of building company owners, he felt like nobody paid attention to the details like he did, but he wasn't going to let that hold him back from becoming a real entrepreneur and building a successful company anymore.

He raised his standards for where his time was best spent, which meant he stopped doing low-level tasks like dealing with email, picking up materials from the hardware store, buying coffees for the boys on the way in, or driving 2 hours every single day to and from the site.

Instead, he focused on becoming a better leader and building a great team so they could carry out the day-to-day operations while he executed on the big picture of the business. Implementing the right hiring and management systems allowed him to step away from the construction site, delegate responsibilities to a team he trusted, and get back a huge amount of time.

His results were even better in the sales and marketing department. After upgrading the marketing systems for his website, Instagram, and dozens of other touchpoints within his sales process, he said, "The number of people ringing and inquiring has been massive."

OUTSTANDING RESULTS

Within 12 months, Dean went from doing $1.5 million per year with slim profits to turning over $8.5 million per year. And now his profitability going into these jobs is about a 20 to 25% margin. To do that all within just 12 months is incredible, and it shows what's possible when you work hard to implement the right systems into every part of your business.

"For 5 years I was a one man band. In our 6th year we employed our first site manager, and I remained as Project Manager, Contracts Admin, Accounts, Estimating and Sales. That grew to two site managers, and I remained as Project Manager, Contracts Admin, Sales and Estimating and I employed an accounts person. That grew to three site managers and three site and I employed a Project Manager I had an account person and I remained in Contracts Admin, Sales and Estimating. Fast forward, we have grown to four site managers and 4 sites and I have a Project Manager, an Accounts Manager and I employed a Contracts Administrator and I remain in sales and estimating."

-Dean W, Brisbane

CHAPTER 6 – SUMMARY

MARKETING TO KEEP YOUR PIPELINE FULL

Sales becomes easier, when marketing does the heavy lifting.

- Understand the **3M's:**

  o Whom your target **Market** are
  o What **Messages** to send and when
  o The different **Mediums** to use for best results

- Your marketing must answer the **4 Key Questions:**

  o Who are you?
  o Who is on your team?
  o Can I trust you?
  o How specifically can you help me?

- How to build your online presence for maximum results.

- Marketing is maths. Use the marketing calculator to determine how much to spend each month to hit your goals.

- How to use your Guarantee to win more projects at a higher margin.

MARKETING TO KEEP YOUR PIPELINE FULL

Sales is easier when marketing does the heavy lifting.
–Marti Amos

When it comes to marketing, the goal is to address your prospects' fears and aspirations and move from being just another residential construction company pricing their project, to being someone's trusted advisor in the build process. You accomplish this by taking people down a funnel of education[1]. This way, as they go through their decision-making process, they move from "I've got a problem" to "What are my potential pains and sources of frustration in building and renovating, and what are the potential solutions?" Then, they wonder, "Who can I choose as my builder to solve these pain points?" After that, they move on to "Who's my ideal builder?"

As time goes on, you're going to capture the people who are ready to make a decision to build or renovate now. With each month that passes, the people who are closer to making a decision are going to be further down the funnel, and in that time, they will have received four, five, seven, or eight emails from you (maybe a postcard and a video showing your build process, how you're the expert, and what they should look out for when building their log cabin, custom home, or doing a remodel). Once someone is far down the decision-making process, you can help them by answering their questions, overcoming their concerns, and pulling back

---

[1] A build is a complex purchase process. Prospects are typically not aware of all the facets and steps involved, (unless they've done a build or a renovation before).

the curtain to show why you are the best option for the biggest investment of their lives.

Make sure your pipeline is full the whole time and nurture the people who want to build or renovate within the next 12 months. A lead generation magnet is a way to capture people's details—those who are interested in what you have to offer. Here are some strategies for each category of prospect, which we'll discuss in more detail throughout the chapter.

> "Working on our marketing systems with TPB changed everything for our sales process. When we go into the first meeting with our clients, they feel like they already know us, and once we bring everything to the table, it's a done deal."

> —Richard P, Timaru

THE MARKETING TRIANGLE

Before you start taking people down your funnel, you need to know the three Ms of marketing: your Market, your Message, and your Medium(s).

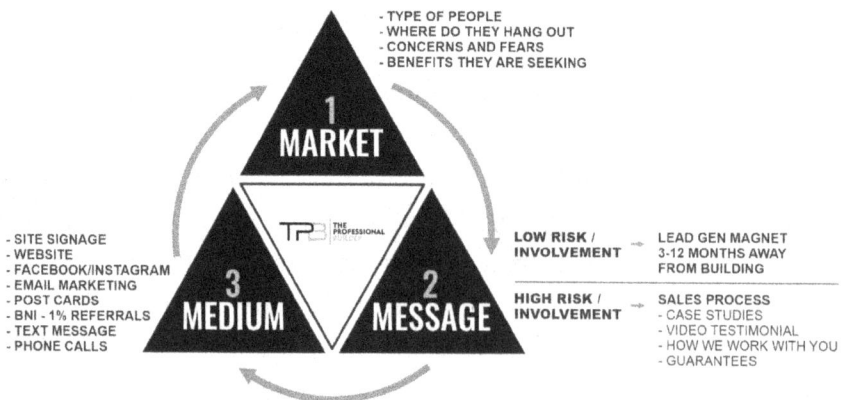

- TYPE OF PEOPLE
- WHERE DO THEY HANG OUT
- CONCERNS AND FEARS
- BENEFITS THEY ARE SEEKING

1 MARKET

TP3 THE PROFESSIONAL

- SITE SIGNAGE
- WEBSITE
- FACEBOOK/INSTAGRAM
- EMAIL MARKETING
- POST CARDS
- BNI - 1% REFERRALS
- TEXT MESSAGE
- PHONE CALLS

3 MEDIUM

2 MESSAGE

LOW RISK / INVOLVEMENT → LEAD GEN MAGNET 3-12 MONTHS AWAY FROM BUILDING

HIGH RISK / INVOLVEMENT → SALES PROCESS
- CASE STUDIES
- VIDEO TESTIMONIAL
- HOW WE WORK WITH YOU
- GUARANTEES

MARKET

What type of people are they?

Understanding your market starts with picking a niche. This doesn't mean that you solely have to build those types of projects (such as villa renovations in Eastern Suburbs). You can still do any other work that comes to you as long as it meets your criteria for the size of the job, where you want to work, the type of people you want to work with, and the right margin. But you do want to specialise and head towards getting booked out with work in the ideal sphere you most want to be known for.

> *"Before TPB, my website was like barren land. We never generated any leads through it. But after working on it for three months with Marti and his team, now people are checking us out online and sending inquiries through our website."*
>
> —Seth A, Nashville

Let's say your chosen niche was sustainable buildings. You could make free eBooks related to eco-friendly building (think of the pain points within that niche and solve those in the content) offered on your website in exchange for email addresses. Put this eBook all around the web. You can market it online and offline. Content like this is going to position you as the expert and allows you to nurture and educate people as they proceed further and move down your funnel and along their buying process. Here are some examples of niche-specific content:

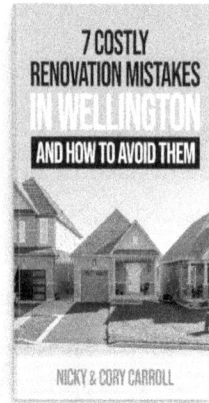

If you are an expert who specialises in something narrow enough, you can become a celebrity within that given community. If you think in terms of doctors, a specialist gets paid more than a general practitioner. And he's going to be the guy who is at the top in terms of premium position, who's booked out months in advance with people (who aren't price sensitive) waiting in line to go and see him, and who is going to be able to command premium prices and get paid what he's worth.

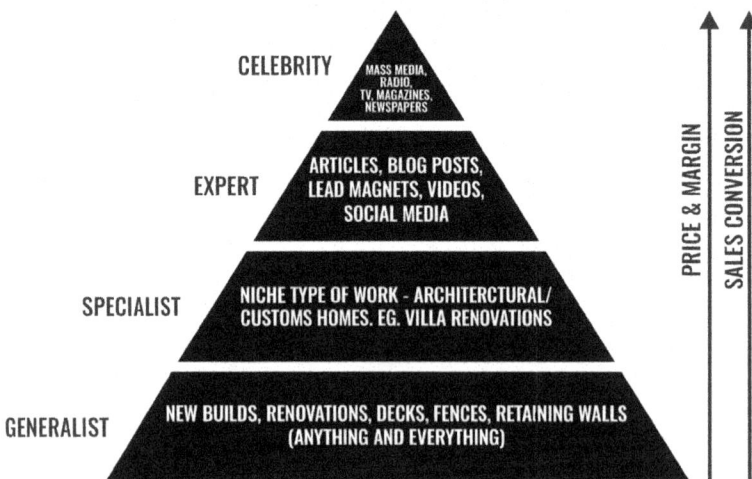

- The same goes with you as a building company owner. To position yourself as the expert, you can:

- Use case studies to show prospects that you've been successful in this niche and are the 'go-to builder' for the type of project they want done (villa renovations, architectural new builds, reclads, etc).

- Use before and after photos and videos to show the quality of work you've done.

Write blogs and value articles specific to that niche.

You can even use any publicity you or your company has had, like TV shows, newspapers, or magazines. For example, among other TV and radio shows, Russ from Licensed Renovations has been featured on BCITO's[2] video campaign called *My Boss: Legend*:

---

[2] BCITO stands for Building and Construction Industry Training Organisation; they train apprentices in New Zealand.

MESSAGE

What are their concerns and fears, and what are the benefits that they're looking for from using you?

In the absence of any other variables and information, people will often use price as their main criteria for choosing a company. This is why you need to demonstrate why your company is the best choice for the biggest investment of their life.

There are 5 key concerns you need to address before, during, and after the project:

1. Budget

2. Timeliness

3. Trustworthiness

4. Quality

5. Communication

This can also be addressed in your own guarantee—which should be in addition to the Master Builder Guarantee or any other association you may be a part of.

Marketing strategies to overcome people's 5 major concerns:

5 POINT GUARANTEE

BUDGET

- Fixed price so no blow outs
- Work with you during the beginning phases to match budget to scope of works so realistic and affordable
- 4 Stage pricing process with our own 55 point pricing checklist to make sure nothing is missing & accurate

TIMELINE

- Work on one job at a time so you are our focus and main priority
- Provide you with a timeline and keep you updated as your job progresses via our project management software
- Dedicated project manager for your project

TRUST

- Homestars
- The Professional Builder member
- Houzz
- 26 years in the industry
- Team with combined 80 years experience
- Only use local suppliers
- 48 completed jobs in the local community over the last 3 Years
- 37 Google 5-star member reviews

QUALITY

- Quality Checklist (287 points)
- Quality seal of approval local supplies
- Trusted quality materials
- Every 6 months we review our vendor's quality and make sure we're getting the best products in the market
- 46 Master Builder Awards

COMMUNICATION

- 24 hour call back policy
- Dedicated team for your project
- Weekly project update and review
- Buildertrend daily updates and photos

Your message should answer the following 4 questions for the prospect so they don't solely judge your company based on price:

The 4 Main Questions

1. Who are you?

2. Who is on your team?

3. How can I trust you?

4. How specifically can you help me?

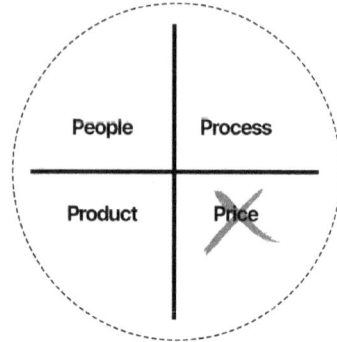

People | Process

Product | Price

These are the 4 main questions you need to answer:

1. Who are you?

The goal is for the client to "Know, Like, and Trust" you. How do you do that? First-person stories will help them get to know you, connection and common ground will get them to like you, and disclosure and honesty will allow them to trust you.

2. Who is on your team?

Describe what each team member's role is on the client's project. They need confidence in your team and systems to get the job done. One thing to remember is that people aren't buying you alone. They are buying the help of your team, partners, and systems. So if you can show them you've got systems and the right team in place to fulfil their project and overcome their concerns, you'll build a strong bond. This can be done via team profiles, photos and videos, rules of the game, and on-site rules.

3. How can you help ME specifically?

Showcase the results you have achieved on similar completed projects and tie them to the person's current situation. You want to let the person know where they're at and how you are the right person to build the biggest investment of their lives.

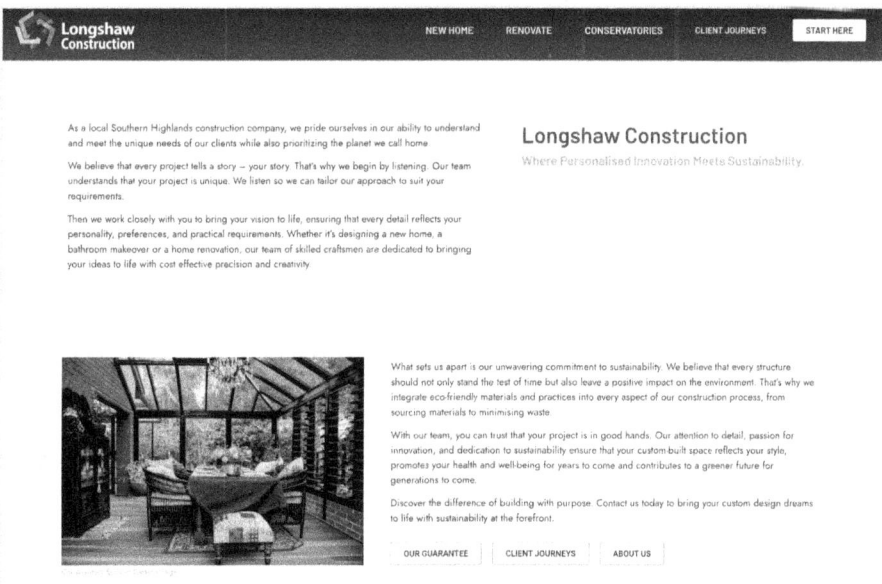

MEDIUM

Where do the people in your market hang out?

- Marketing is all about education and communication. Your market needs to know

- what's available for them before, during, and after the build.

- why they should choose you over any other builder.

- what the features, advantages, and benefits are of using your company instead of another builder.

- how to go about choosing you, i.e. the next steps in your process.

Build a marketing system and have sequential marketing that is available through different mediums. Some people will be visual, so they'll prefer online marketing or social media. Your online marketing should include Google Ads set up to appear on different websites, Facebook ads with effective calls to action, Instagram stories of your projects and a LinkedIn page with the right look and way to contact you. In fact, your online marketing could look similar to this:

Surfing the Web
- Banner Ad Placements
- Google Display Network
- Youtube Video

Social Media Marketing
- Facebook Marketing
- Linkedin Marketing
- Instagram
- TikTok

Actively Searching
- Google Adwords
- Search Engine Optimisation

Actively Searching
- Google Adwords
- Search Engine Optimisation

Your Website
Landing Pages
Targeted Conversion
Strategies

Take Action — *No Action Taken*

Online Marketing Strategy
- Conversion tracking
- Split testing
- Monthly KPI tracking
- Ongoing optimisation.
- Strategy adjustment

Remarketing Banners

SOCIAL TRAFFIC

There are 2 main ways to get traffic from social media like Facebook, Instagram, YouTube, LinkedIn, etc.: organic and paid. The most reliable way to get in front of new people is using paid ads to get your message in front of the right people.

LEAD MAGNET EXAMPLE

XYZ Builder
Sponsored

Like Page

Want to avoid the painful headaches you've heard horror stories about when it comes to your new custom home? Download our "8-Step Guide to avoiding costly overruns and nightmare mistakes when building your dream home in [xyz suburb]"

HIT A PAIN POINT
Specific End Benefit if possible
Strong Call-to-Action

7 COSTLY RENOVATION MISTAKES IN WELLINGTON AND HOW TO AVOID THEM

EYE CATCHING
Portrays the message
What is it?!

What is it?

Use the How We Work With You Template & E-Book Training To Build Your E-Book Offer To Get More Leads

XYZ BUILDER.COM

DOWNLOAD

Reiterate the Call-to-Action.

When driving traffic from social media, the two most effective ways are:

1. To a free resource, which could be a PDF guide, ebook, checklist, or any other information your potential clients might find useful.

2. Directly to an offer for a free consultation.

When it comes to getting traffic from search engines, you have the same two options: organic and paid.

Organic traffic depends on where you naturally appear in the Google search results and how well-optimised your Google Business Profile is. Paid traffic is achieved using Google Ads (formerly Google Adwords) to appear at the top of the search results for certain keywords, retargeting, and your social media profile posts.

For search engine traffic, the key secret to better conversions is sending people to a webpage that is focused on what they were searching for. For example, if someone was searching for "villa renovations," you should send them to a landing page that is all about your villa renovation services.

Once you have a free resource to give away, you can include it on your landing pages. When someone wants to download your free resource, they simply click the link to your free resource landing page and enter their name, email, and phone number.

Once they click submit, two things should happen:

1. They get added to your email marketing system, which sends them an email with a link to the resource they requested (you should also get notified of the new lead so you can give them a call).

2. The visitor should be taken to a thank you page, confirming the resource will be in their inbox shortly and also offering them a free consultation that spells out the process and the benefits of meeting with you.

If they are interested in a consultation, they fill in the application and, optionally, book a time to speak with them.

Here's an example of a free resource landing page:

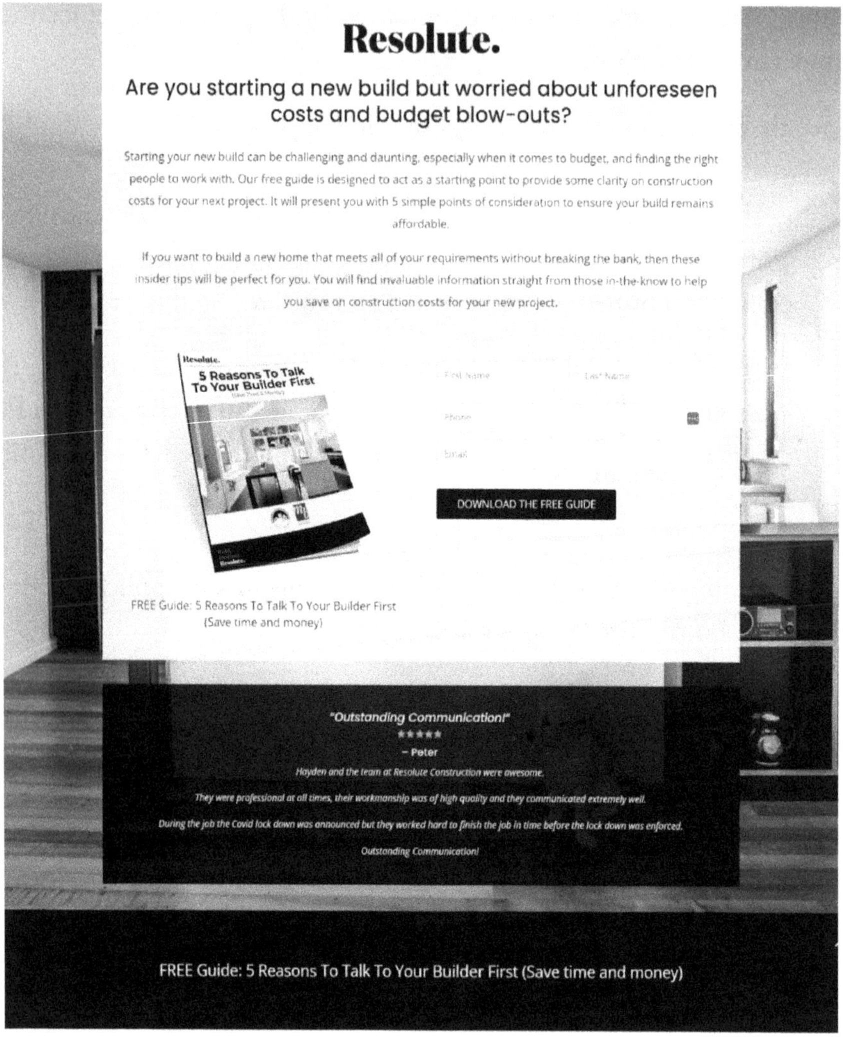

Also, here is an example of an individual service landing page:

Be sure to include plenty of video testimonials that highlight what your guarantee is. By doing this, you can also have a How We Work With You video that goes behind the scenes, pulls back the curtain, and shows customers the 287-point quality assurance checklist, the systems, the processes that you have, and how your project management works to ensure you can deliver on their scope of work and budget.

TARGET THE RIGHT PEOPLE WITH LEAD GENERATION MAGNETS AND VALUE

When generating leads, it's important to remember that not everyone is ready to buy now, and that's a great opportunity to nurture them for when they are ready. There are people who might be looking to start their project within the next three, six, nine, or twelve months from the time they are seeking the information, and that's a chance for you to warm them up. Most people only target the people who are ready to buy now and don't develop a funnel of consistent leads to warm up.[3] This is where the gold in your list is.

PURCHASERS TIME PYRAMID—THE BUYERS TRIANGLE

5% READY NOW

READY RIGHT NOW!
PUT THROUGH THE 10-STEP SALES PROCESS

25% 3 - 12 MONTHS AWAY

- EDUCATE
- NURTURE
- QUALIFY
- KNOW, LIKE, TRUST
- PRELIM BUDGET PROCESS

70% NOT INTERESTED

RETARGET (LEAD MAGNETS)
- ARTICLES
- BLOGS
- 1% REFERRAL

---

[3] If you are only dealing with people who are at the sharp end (the top of the funnel) and ready to make a decision, then you're typically going to be competing on price against 2 - 3 other builders.

Roughly 5% are ready to make a decision right now. The funny thing is that this is where most people are focused—just on this 5%. The problem is that they miss out on all the people who might be 3 to 12 months away, which would be 25% of the market[4]. Doing a build is a high-involvement decision, which typically means high risk and high consideration[5]; a lot of things can go wrong. So, you want to build a relationship with these people and gain their trust over time.

Lastly, you have the people who might have been looking but aren't really serious, which is 70% of the market. The thing to remember is that even if they're not looking, they may have friends who are looking to do a renovation since people tend to hang around those who are of similar social standing and mindset.

> "Before I joined TPB, I had a bad financial year. I was struggling to find new jobs. We didn't have a solid marketing system in place. Marti helped build our website, and we got 11 leads in 10 days. Now we're booked out for the next 9 months."
>
> –Brendon S, Auckland

MARKETING IS MATHS

If you know what the numbers are at each step of the marketing funnel and sales process, you can make improvements to every single step. To do this, you need to know how many leads you are getting each month, how many of those convert to a site visit, and how many of those convert to pricing the job.

If you get twelve leads a month, six site visits, quote three prices, and win two jobs, then one opportunity to improve is how your website and

---

[4] The real gold is in those who are 3 to 12 months away from making a decision. They enter our world aware of a problem.
[5] A low involvement (low-risk) purchase is where you might go to the supermarket, you buy a packet of chewing gum. High involvement (high-risk) purchase is a big dollar investment in which there's a big downside if things go wrong.

marketing attracts people who are interested in your service. You can do that with phone scripts and qualifying text on your website. You might even need to have a more direct Call to Action, such as "Call Ross right now at 5556789 to discuss how we can turn your dreams into reality."

If you generate leads consistently with your marketing machine, you might get 20 to 30 leads a month. Then, choose which seven or eight jobs are in your sweet spot to price. Then, choose the two or three in which you can have your ideal gross profit margin and the right type of clients you want to work with.

To figure out how many leads you need, work out how much your ideal lifestyle costs per year.[6] Let's say it's $500,000, and your overheads are $200,000. In this case, you need to make $700,000 in total gross profit, which at a 20% gross profit would require you to do $3.5 million in sales and an average dollar sale value of $100,000 with 35 projects at this rate.

Always migrate to bigger jobs that are in your sweet spot, where you can control the margin. For example, if you know you have to get to $3.5m, and you grow to doing $350,000 average dollar job projects, you now only need to do 10 jobs during the year. $700,000 average project size means you now only need to complete 5 projects.

> "After 90 days of working on our sales process with Marti, we qualified 23 leads, and then the next month, we started charging for our quotes. It's amazing knowing we get paid for pricing jobs even if they decide not to move forward."
>
> –Darren M, Cambridge

---

[6] Throughout the marketing process, you need to clarify your *why*. You can use our Dream Builder and our Vision Book to do this. I do mine every year at Christmas time with my wife, Kelly. She helps motivate me and makes me say, "Hey, how are we doing? Are we buying that new house next year? Are we going on holiday to Europe?" So, every time I come home, I have some extra motivation.

MARKETING CALCULATOR

The marketing budget calculator will help you work out how to "reverse engineer" what you need to spend on marketing to hit your revenue and profit goal. Your conversion rate[7] depends on how strong your marketing is and how good your sales process is. If you have different marketing sources, you're going to have a lower conversion rate but much higher average sales and much higher revenue than if you solely relied on word of mouth (hope is not a strategy).

If your conversion rate is 20%, to hit your ideal lifestyle goal, you would need 25 leads. If it were 10%, you would need 50 leads.

To understand exactly how many leads you need to meet your goals, we have built the Marketing Budget Calculator.

What do you need to fund your ideal lifestyle 12 months from now? Make sure your profit is over and above your salary (your salary should be included in your overheads—it's part of your total fixed costs). Fill in what your desired profit is at the top where it says Annual Sales Goal. Next, below that, there's Revenue. How much revenue do you need to do (and so on)?

---

[7] The number of leads divided by the number of contracts signed.

Marketing Budget Calculator

Annual Sales Goal	$ 6,000,000
Enter Your Average Sale Value (total sales no. of jobs done):	$ 800,000
Number of Projects You Need to Complete each Year	7.5
Enter Your Conversion Rate (no. of jobs won/no. of quotes done)	50%
Number of QUALIFIED leads You Require to quote Annually:	**15.0**
Number of total leads. (Double it)	30.0
Total leads per month	2.5
Cost per lead	$ 1,000.00
Total advertising spend	**$ 30,000**
Management fee if paying someone (Monthly)	$ 0
Total Marketing Budget (Annual)	$ 30,000
Total Marketing Budget (Monthly)	$ 2,500
Cost per client	$ 4,000
Gross Margin	**20%**
Gross Profit	**$ 1,200,000**
Return on ad spend (Gross Profit) (ie. Put $1 in the machine and get this back)	**$ 40.00**
Return on ad spend (Net Profit)	**$20.00**

TESTING

Test and measure where your business is going and how your marketing is performing. Online marketing can be done cheaply from $3000 and you can scale it up to $200,000 per month or year. You can test and measure the return you're getting each month. You can start investing more in Google Ads, social media (Facebook, Instagram, or TikTok), and your website (the main retail storefront where you will generate leads). You need to track and measure your return on investment and cost per acquisition[8] with each avenue to make sure you know how many leads you need from each source to hit your goals.

Now, going forward, if you need to create 50 leads, come up with 2-3 strategies to create 15-20 for each. The next step is to break this down by month. If you're going to work 10 months out of the year, then you need 5 leads per month.

---

[8] The cost to acquire one client.

After that, measure how many leads you get from a particular medium. This way, you know which marketing strategies are working well and which ones aren't. Check this weekly and monthly. Ideally, you'll want to make this visible for everyone to see on a leads/sales whiteboard/ spreadsheet during your weekly meetings with your team.

BUILDER'S ROADMAP TIP

If you got twelve leads during the month, and you know that nine of them came from site signage and three of them came from Google Ads, the next step is to work out what the dollar amount that you spent on each of these was. Then you can determine your cost per lead source and how much you are spending to generate a lead. Then you can work out how many leads you need and how much money you need to spend each month.

If you need 10 leads and are spending $250 a lead, then you've spent $2,500 a month to get those 10 leads, of which maybe four won't qualify to work with you. Six who you talk to, you may progress to a site visit. Then out of those six, you might quote three to win one job. So, if that one job is $250,000, you know that $2,500 is what your client acquisition cost is. So, for $250 a lead, you get ten leads, which results in one client each month at $250,000.

> *"Before I met Marti, I was taking what I could get. But now our marketing machine is generating lots of leads and it allowed me to be more selective in terms of meeting new clients. We've bumped up our average project value, and the margin is above 20%."*
>
> —Sean W, Christchurch

You can also test, for example, what your best-performing headline, image, or offer is. If you were doing postcards, for example, you could do three different batches of 5000 postcards, each batch with a distinct headline, image, or offer. You can then see which of those variations is going to work best. With online marketing, you can test this very quickly through Facebook, YouTube, Instagram, and Google Ads, and you can track your metrics right on the website/in the app.

You can also have two separate landing pages that someone visits; one has headline A, and one has headline B, but the rest of the page is the same. Split testing the effectiveness of each headline using this method is pretty straightforward and a great place to start.

50%
of visitors
see variation A

50%
of visitors
see variation B

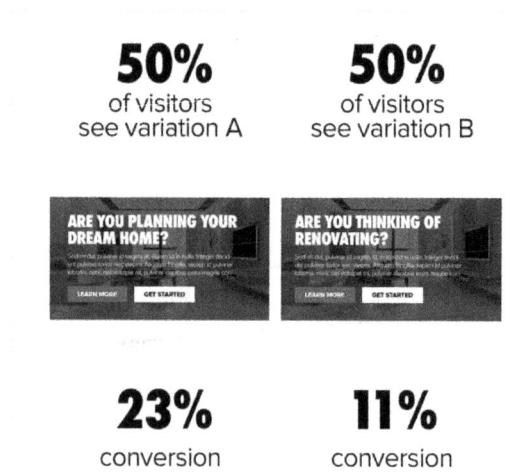

23%
conversion

11%
conversion

With this data, you know what your metrics are and can, therefore, decide if you want to scale that up. It will also help you decide which steps you want to improve; without these numbers, you are just guessing.

> *"We followed your marketing systems, and now we're number one on Google. People get to our website. They sent us an inquiry. Straight away, they receive an automatic survey. They fill that out, qualifying themselves without us lifting a finger."*
>
> —Dave H, Sydney

GET RAVING FANS—NOT JUST REFERRALS BY DEFAULT

All of this research, planning, and testing leads to the sales process, which we have refined as part of the Builder's Blueprint and outlined in the following chapter for you to use, complete with downloads, scripts, and a repeatable process that converts. But first, we need to go over referrals and how to get high-quality ones.

This is how your marketing flows into your sales process:

The objective in sales is to educate suspects to become prospects, nurture prospects to become customers, and then build trust throughout the business relationship so that they become repeat customers. Repeat customers then become "raving fans," which means they will refer you to more people.

THE PROFESSIONAL BUILDER'S 1% REFERRAL SYSTEM

We have a referral system you can put into place to ensure a steady stream of work that flows from your current network: the TPB 1% Referral System. Your raving fans get 1% of the value of the contract for the build once it's signed and the deposit is paid. What you can do is create a top list of people you could reach out to, it can be past clients, friends, family, or colleagues who might know someone who would be a good prospect for a project with your company.

The next step is to map out what you are going to give them. How much should you give away? It needs to be enough to incentivise someone to go out of their way and directly refer you to someone in their network. Whenever you refer someone, your reputation is at stake. So we want to do everything we can to put their minds at ease and show them they have chosen the right company to refer to, and that their referral is in safe hands. Like I mentioned before, typically, you may give away 1% of the total value of the project. So if someone refers a $500,000 project to you, you're going to give away $5000 to the referrer.

Simpson Residential Ltd

Give Away

Receive one of these desirable gifts when you recommend a referral to Simpson Residential and it leads to a signed building contract.

It's that easy!

GIFT ONE

GIFT TWO

Punakaiki Resort

REWARD VALUE $500

Receive 1 nights accommodation for two + Dinner at The Club Bar & Jacobs Grill Restaurant

Recommend a referral which leads to a New Build or Renovation contract valued at $50,000 and this will be yours!

Domestic Air New Zealand Voucher

REWARD VALUE $1,500

If your recommendation leads to a New Build or Renovation contract valued at $150,000 you will instantly receive a $1,500 Air NZ Voucher to be used on a domestic destination of your choice!

With a substantial referral system in place, your existing clients (the ones you now have the freedom to cherry-pick as a profitable selective building company) bring on more of your ideal kind of clients. The ones in your top 20% of clients, keep refining your ideal clients as you go, and you have better clients as time goes by.

> *"Before TPB, we were lucky to get 2 leads for a house in a year from referrals. Now, we have a referral system running, and we're pulling in 8 solid leads a month. It's [a] night and day difference."*
>
> —Jesse B, British Columbia

BUILDER'S ROADMAP TIP:

IMPROVE THE QUALITY OF YOUR PROSPECTS BY RATING YOUR CURRENT AND PAST CLIENTS.

- To ensure you have great client experiences, you must know what kind of clients you want. Rank your past and current clients as either A, B, C, or D. You want to make sure you are getting more of the A-grade type of clients. These might be people who
- are doing high-end renovations that are between $500,000 and $800,000.
- need to start work within the next three to six months.
- live within a 5-10km radius.

Analyse how prospects compare with your best clients to determine whether or not you can take them on. Focusing your energy and resources on the *right* prospects will provide you with a steady flow of ongoing work so you can be booked out six to twelve months in advance at a great gross profit margin (20% or above).

Now, of course, to get the right people, you've got to find them in the right places. We talked about generating leads, but how do you specifically find these people?

Now, before we even talk about your sales process, think about how your company looks to the prospect. If you want better-quality clients, you have to become a better-quality company, on the inside and the outside. There are so many things that communicate to the prospect your level of expertise and professionalism.

> *"We've gone from getting all of our work from word of mouth to generating our own leads. Marti and the team helped us build our marketing machine, and it has been filling our pipeline with high-value projects. Knowing that we're booked months in advance really helped relieve the weight off our shoulders."*

–James F, Morden

BECOME A BETTER QUALITY COMPANY

To boost sales, you need to play a bigger game. In order to play a bigger game, you need to invest in yourself, your business, and your team. This means you're going to have to spend some more money/time—in targeted areas—to maximise your success.

- Now that you understand what you need to have in place to market your business and how to get the best referrals, I leave you with some things you can do to help your company's professionalism that will boost sales. I highly suggest implementing at least one of these tips every 90 days:

- If your team has grown, you're going to want to spend a little bit more on clothes and uniforms. Your merchant may be willing to fund at least 50% (if not more) of on-site signage, vehicle signage, and uniforms for your company in exchange for exposure to your market and the possibility of more referrals from you.

- You might need to hire an office manager, which might be a salary of $50,000 - $85,000.

- You may need to shift to a bigger office with a warehouse at the back to store gear and materials.

- Your salary might go up from, say, $87,000 to $125,000, and you may want to invest in yourself in terms of coaching and mentoring for the year to get there faster, so you might need to invest in yourself and that business training, which then gets allocated to your fixed costs.

- You could better define your unique selling proposition (USP).[9] Why would someone choose you over any of the other building companies out there?

- You can put the TPB 1% Referral System into action in order to get a lot more *targeted* leads in. You could use this to position your company as the go-to builder within your chosen niche.

- Nail down your niche as well. Are you being all things to everyone? It's best to focus on the one niche you are best at. This will inevitably drive sales at higher conversion rates and profit margins.

- You might seek to improve your cost of sales by regularly talking with your current subcontractors and negotiating with other subcontractors.

- You can also make sure your guys are hitting their milestones by incentivising them. Measure their labour hours (their *productive* hours), comparing their actual hours to the forecast hours at every stage of the project to ensure there's no excess there.

You can improve your pricing to get a higher gross profit margin (including project management fees).

If you implement some (or all) of these strategies into your business, you will improve your leads and your profits, just like countless others who have used the strategies housed within the Builder's Roadmap. These proven strategies build trust and accountability in what you have to offer, which will drive the right people to you—the ones who will make the most difference in your business.

---

9 The thing that makes your company better than your competitors.

ACTION STEPS

1. Hire a marketing coordinator for 10 hours or more per week and answer the 4 Questions and 5 Key Concerns clients have.

2. Plan your guarantee and put it on your direct response website.

3. Film a How We Work With You Video and film 3 video testimonials.

4. Implement the TPB 1% referral system

We have all of the marketing materials for you to put this referral system into play today, including a PDF and step-by-step scripts for you to use.

Scan the code for all the resources:

MEMBER PROFILE: MARK T.

Before joining The Professional Builder, Mark always chased the dollar and took on any work that came knocking on his door. He thought this was how successful building company owners grew their businesses by taking on more projects and doing free stuff to get his name out there.

But after years of sticking to the same plan, his numbers weren't improving. He was still cutting his price to win jobs, and his cash flow took a big hit. He would have restless nights wondering if he had enough money to pay his guys and fund the new jobs.

Mark knew he was a great builder and wanted a profitable business where his clients paid him what he was worth. He envisioned becoming the go-to builder in his local area but didn't know how to do it. He felt other guys knew secrets he was unaware of. But when he joined us, he discovered it all boils down to systems.

So, we focused our effort on the marketing machine checklist to position Mark as the builder of choice and attract his ideal clients.

First, we defined his perfect lead and unique selling proposition. Then, we worked on creating a high-converting website where he could drive his leads and give them confidence prior to having a phone call. After launching his website, the right type of projects started flowing in, and the response was overwhelmingly positive. His project pipeline began to fill up with high-value clients. Within 4 months, he was fully booked for a year and still receives referrals for bigger projects with margins above 20%.

In Mark's words: "It's a good feeling to choose what I want to work on next."

CHAPTER 7 – SUMMARY
THE 10 STEP SALES PROCESS

Have a sales process that consistently converts prospects to profitable projects.

- Map out and systemise each step of your sales process so you only deal with your ideal clients and qualify out the time wasters.

- Send a WOW Info Pack in advance of your site visits to educate and nurture your prospects.

- Charge for your Quote/Preliminary Budget and stop giving away your time and expertise for free.

- Use the High Converting Action Plan to win projects at a higher margin.

THE 10-STEP SALES PROCESS THAT CONSISTENTLY CONVERTS

Sales is easier when marketing does the heavy lifting and pre-sells people on why they should choose you.
–Marti Amos

WHAT'S YOUR CURRENT SALES CONVERSION RATE?

Ninety days from now, what do you *want* that conversion rate to be?

A good target would be at least 50%—five out of ten projects that you price. Any more than that, and you might be leaving quite a bit of money on the table trying to do it all and cut costs, or maybe you're getting most of your jobs by referrals, and *those* people are converting well. But referrals should be the cherry on top, not the whole cake itself. Most of your prospects should be coming from direct response marketing, strategic alliances with architects, site signage, and other online and offline marketing strategies.

> *"One of the biggest things TPB helped me establish is our sales process. We've implemented a whole system, a step-by-step process from lead generation right through to contract signing. We've got a process in place that we know we have to follow every step and get that process done, so it becomes repeatable, it becomes consistent, and it becomes a huge conversion rate changer.*

Our conversion rate before TPB was sitting around 30%, we're now higher up near 60%. Before we've even submitted a quote, the clients have already invested in us as a builder, as a building company, and we've won the job 60% of the time before we've even issued the quote to them.

Because of the sales process that we implemented, we were able to improve our conversion rate from 30% to 60% and we make most of those sales prior to even pricing the job. By implementing the sales process, we were able to double our conversion rate on our sales. So another good system and process that we put in place."

—Simon M, Sydney

"We charge $3,500 for quotes, and we implemented exactly what TPB has taught us to do. It's been working like a charm. We charged seven clients for quotes and closed all of them; one was a $1.2M job."

—Leon G, Melbourne

"This week we solidified just over $200k of work, with another $200k-$250k to be confirmed in the next two weeks, and another ~$1.5m-$2m in the pipeline.

—Alex H, Texas

"About to lock in $990k, $1.4m, and $880k projects, all at a minimum of 25% margins, with 3 more jobs being quoted in the pipeline—business is growing well!

—Stewart G, Florida

> *"We have doubled in size from last year, and with TPB's systems we created a great team. To top it off, I don't work weekends and spend Wednesday working on my own home!*
>
> — Hayden S, Hokitika

What's going to make the biggest difference in your conversion rate is the confidence that a clear, mapped-out sales process brings. Here's how the sales process for a residential building company should flow:

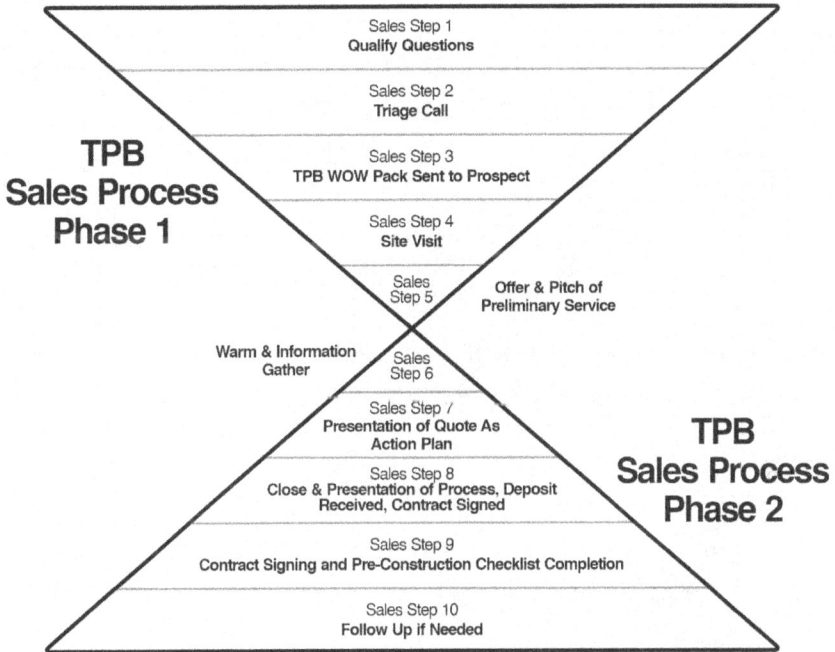

You need something that works every time. The following process has been refined over the last 21 years with over 2,500+ business owners. The Professional Builder's Sales Process will allow you to have a consistent deal flow (with the right clients) and increase your profits.

THE PROFITABLE BUILDER'S SALES PROCESS

This is the precise process that our member, Hayden, used to secure four projects valued at $4,100,000 and payment for three preliminary budgets at $3,500 each, over the course of six weeks.

> *Currently, I'm not working in the business anymore. I'm focused on property development and spec builds, stepping in only when there's an emergency. I leave everything else to the foreman. They report to me, and I visit them three times a week. This arrangement is possible because we have systems in place like the A-Z of operations and the 287 Checklist. I just give the foreman the parameters, things to inspect, and the deadlines for each stage.*
>
> — Hayden N, Waikanae

1. Make the Initial Contact With Your Prospect as Professional as Possible

When a prospect gets in touch with you, get their phone number and address. Chat with them to understand what they want to achieve.

After getting their contact details, you always call the prospective client first. The main goal here is to touch base, build rapport, and send the qualifying questionnaire. Don't waste time talking specifics about the project; all we want them to do is to fill out our questionnaire.

Here's an initial phone conversation script that you can use:

Initial Phone Script Questionnaire

Hi {name},

Tessa here from _____. Is now a good time to talk? Great! Well, firstly, thank you for inquiring with _____. We really appreciate you taking the time to get in touch.

Are you looking to build or renovate? Great.

In order for me to help you best, I will need some more information. We have a brief questionnaire that takes about 5 - 10 minutes to complete. However, it will give us a good overview of your project plans and see where we can help.

Once we have received your completed questionnaire, _____ will absorb the information. Then he will give you a call to have a meaningful conversation about your project and what it is you want to achieve.

Could I please get your email address and I will send you the questions now.

It has been lovely speaking with you and we look forward to receiving your completed questionnaire.

Bye!

2. Send Your Prospect a Qualifying Questionnaire

Rather than work with time wasters or people whose scope of work doesn't fit their budget, you want to qualify those people out. A qualifying questionnaire will save you from time wasters and serves as an autoresponder funnel to help warm up the people who are three, six, nine, or twelve months away from building. You can attract these people with a lead generation magnet that is going to position you as the expert. This lead generation magnet might be a free ebook you're giving out in exchange for their details, for example, *Top Nine Things You Need to Know Before Renovating Your Villa*.

If you're just popping around the next day and you're going, "Oh yeah, to build your house, it'll be about four thousand dollars per square metre", how professional is that? As opposed to the following:

"Hey, Mr. and Mrs. Prospect. Before our founder comes out to see you at the site visit, we're going to send you a questionnaire so he knows a little bit more about you. This way, he can help you best when he comes out to see you."

Here is Hayden's questionnaire:

Project Information

| Are you the legal owner of the property? | ○ Yes | ○ No |
| | ○ Yes - its in trust | |

What type of home are you wanting	○ Forever Home	
	○ Family Home	
	○ Bach	
	○ Town Houses	
	○ Other ▼	

| Have you Built before? | ○ Yes | |
| | ○ No | |

Have you selected an Architect/Designer	○ Yes	
	○ No	
	○ Would like to use Resolute Design service	

| Has Resource Consent been approved? | ○ Yes | ○ No |
| | ○ Not sure if required | ○ Not applicable |

| Has Building Consent been approved? | ○ Yes | ○ No |
| | ○ Not sure if required | ○ Not applicable |

| Do you have finance | ○ Yes | ○ No |
| | ○ I would like help from Resolute Construction with finance | |

Please select anything you would like help or advice with	○ Electrical Layout	○ Kitchen Design
	○ Products & Fittings	○ Landscaping
	○ Interior Design	○ Other ▼

| Would you like to purchase any items yourself for the build | ○ Yes | |
| | ○ No - I would like to take advantage of Resolute Construction's buying power to save money | |

If yes, what items would you like to purchase yourself?

[ ]

How soon would you like the build to start

○ As soon as possible
○ 3 - 6 Months
○ 6 - 12 Months
○ 12+ Months

What is the estimated budget for the project?

○ $0 - $500k
○ $500k - $1M
○ $1M - $2M
○ $2M+

What else has to happen before the building work can start?

[ ]

How did you hear about us?

[ ]

Upload any plans or files here

Choose files or drag here

Next

3. Send Out a "WOW" Info Pack to the Prospect

1. Warm people up and educate your prospects so they go from cold to pre-sold and then from pre-sold to sold. Sales become easier when marketing does the heavy lifting. Your "WOW" Info Pack helps to differentiate you from the competitors. People look at it, and it answers the four key questions mentioned in the last chapter that every person has prior to choosing a builder:

2. Who are you?

3. What's your company about?

4. Can I trust you?

5. How specifically can you help me?

Check out Leon's results when he incorporated his "WOW" Info Pack into the sales process:

LG BUILDING

Leon started charging for quotes and closed 7/7 proposals, collecting $30K+ for pricing work.

In this info pack, include your guarantee. So what is your company guarantee?[1] You might guarantee no yucky stuff on site. No swearing, no loud radios, no dogs. You might guarantee, "We'll leave your home cleaner than we found it." If you're doing renovations, a big one is: "Our guys use drop sheets." You may do all of these things, but are you communicating them to your target market?[2]

5. Schedule a Site Visit

Once you've sent out the info pack, book the on-site visit as soon as you can. You want to make sure that all the decision-makers (usually the two spouses) are present.

---

[1] Most people are concerned about budget—about whether the job actually finishes on time or goes over budget. Video testimonials are great for showing that you actually stay within the time frame and under budget. You can say, "We guarantee you'll get $117 for every day that we are over." Or if someone has a fixed-price contract, you can guarantee, "It won't be anything over this, unless you make a variation or order change." (Make sure you're getting any variations signed off before proceeding. It's also part of the sales process to really make the prospects understand the variations process.)

[2] You've got to overcome people's concerns with your guarantee. If you get this right, you'll increase your sales, increase your conversion, increase your margin, land bigger jobs, gain trust quicker, and of course, make more profit. People move faster to get away from pain than they do towards pleasure.

Have your whole team there as well: your project manager, surveyor, QS/estimator, foreman, and any of your sub-trades who are going to be on-site for the project. This way, your prospects can see that there's a whole team behind their project, which will give them greater confidence that their project has your team's full attention.

With all of this effort up front, we want the prospect to think, "Wow! They are so thorough *before* they even start the job. Imagine how professional and well-systemised they will be *during* the job." After all, a building project is the biggest investment in most people's lives. So, this is where it really pays to differentiate yourself from the other builders out there, the ones who are just putting out a quote or slapping out, "Yeah, that should be right, dude. It'll be about…three and a half thousand dollars a square metre."

> *"Ever since we started working with Marti, we have been winning projects left and right even though we weren't the cheapest. They said we were the most professional out of all the options, and they wanted us to build their new homes."*
>
> –Paul B, Auckland

6. Warmup/Triage Script

Once they return the questionnaire, you've got to have a second high-performing script that will ensure you've got all the prospects involved (usually spouses) committed to the next step, which is to work out the preliminary costs.

For those who don't qualify (perhaps they don't have the budget or a compatible time frame/expectation), you can archive them. They can join your mailing list or receive updates on projects you are doing, tips, case studies, etc. We want to generate interest so that they come back to you when they're ready to build. If they don't qualify at all, have a script ready for that as well and refer them to a suitable person.

7. Work Out the Preliminary Costs in a Meeting

For the setting of this meeting, it's best for them to come to your office. If they have kids, and it's actually easier for you to go to their place, it's usually best to do so at the end of the day. If you don't have an office, you have no options. You're better off going to their house than going to a cafe.

But before going through with the process of giving your qualified prospect a full quote, at this meeting, you want to talk about the budget.

Let's say their budget is $500,000, for example. By the time you take off the goods and services tax (GST), any other taxes, the council fees (planning, zoning, and building), the permit, the kitchen, and a roof, you might find they haven't got enough money to achieve what they want in their scope.

You've got to qualify your client at the start with their budget, too.

> *"Over the last three months, I've been putting a lot of focus on refining my sales process and it paid off! We quoted $45,000 more than other builders and the client still went with us. It gets easy to land profitable jobs with the systems Marti gave me."*
>
> –Joey H, Canada

If you sense the possibility of a higher budget, to add some urgency to your offer, you could say, "Look, you are aware of what's happening in the market. The best thing we can do to give you the most cost-effective build is to get on with it. The sooner you sign the contract and make decisions, the sooner we can start ordering materials. I've got clients who're still going through resource consent.[3] They've only got draft concept plans, but they're already at the plumber's merchants, choosing fittings and stuff." Of course, you've got to get the materials to follow through with this tactic, but the sooner you know it's coming up, the sooner you can order them. Once the project starts, the client will likely reconsider a higher budget.

---

[3] Permission by the New Zealand government to use natural and physical resources.

They want their dream build to happen and by showing how important it is to you, they know you want to make it happen for them and will respond accordingly.

8. Charge for Your Quote/Prelim Budget.

Once you know what your prospect is willing to pay and they qualify to work with you, you can go ahead with determining an actual quote for the work. You want to be paid for this step in the process—it takes up your valuable time. You've got to do it right by hiring a QS/Estimator or doing it yourself, and getting professional quotes from your own subcontractors, so it's only fair. Don't eat that cost.

TOP PRICING TIP

CHARGE FOR QUOTES

- Stop doing free quotes!
- Charge for your QS's time - make him a valued team member in your business ...do this especially if You are the QS
- E.g. $1,200-$3,500 per quote
- There is a process for being able to position yourself to do this — starting with improving your:

  - Marketing
  - Website
  - Information Pack
  - Scripts
  - Paperwork

TPB THE PROFESSIONAL BUILDER

Examples of pages from a high converting quote template:

MONTHLY FINANCIAL

Your monthly meeting will be an opportunity to examine your budget and how the job is tracking. We can reflect on the previous stage of the build and tell you our plan for the next.

CHANGE ORDERS

In many cases during the concept and construction drawing stages, the builder, Quantity Surveyor or architect would have made allowances for things like your tapware, kitchen cabinets and other items. These are what are known as prime cost items and provisional sums.

The selections stage takes an enormous amount of time and unfortunately some clients leave this till the last minute and end up pressured into making the wrong decisions. Get a head start early and have a look at what you like. If you make early selections, you can give these to your builder to add to the estimate for better accuracy. If you wait, then the builder will generally dictate the terms of the Prime Cost Items.

At Dimension Building, we have an interior designer who helps our clients with everything, from kitchen designs through to tiles and tapware selections - all within the allotted budget set by our Proposal.

The sheet pictured outlines the dates in which you need to have your selections chosen for each stage of your build to ensure a smooth timeline and no work stoppages.

If you need help with any selections or an ear to talk through your ideas please reach out to Summer (summer@dimensionbuilding.co.nz) and she will be more than happy to help."

BUILDER TREND

Buildertrend is a great tool for both clients and their building team to be able to keep track of their build both financially and progress stages. When your profile is created in Buildertrend you will get an invite via email to be able to view your build and keep track.

The email will be the one used in your Master Builder Contract. Once you receive the invite please accept it and log in to track your build.
We will help you set this up at our pre-construction meeting."

FOUNDATIONS & FLOOR

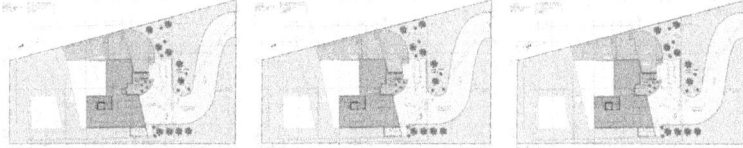

EXCAVATION

A PC SUM of $21,768.25 has been provided for the excavation works at ███████ Paul Smith Earthmoving (PSE) to Undertake Works As per schedule:

Breakout and remove existing retaining wall 18m2 @ $63.00	$1,134.00
Breakout any existing pavements / demolish an existing infrastructure 1 LS	$1,700.00
Excavate all topsoil (approx. depth 300mm) from the site and stockpile 1143 m2 @ $3.50	$4,000.50
Cut to Waste - rate only 200 m3 @ $27.50	$5,500.00
Cut to Fill - rate only 125 m3 @ $31.00	$3,875.00
Import pitrun or suitable material to bring site to desired levels- rate only 1 m3 @ $85.00	$85.00
Import pitrun or suitable material and place as engineered fill to underside of structural Concrete & Ribraft slab - Allowed 150mm AP65 35.25 m3 @ $85.00	$2,996.25
Import and place 25mm sand blinding - 118 m2 @ $12.50	$1,475.00
800mm x 200mm dp Foundation Wing Wall 3.5lm @ $65.00	$227.50
400x400x000mm Post Hole 1 each @ $75.00	$75.00
Allow to prep the underside of the oustide concrete patio area 20m2 @ $35	$700.00
TOTAL PC SUM	$21,768.25

QUALIFICATIONS
- Prices subject to final levels found on site during construction
- PSE require unhindered access to the worksite
- Prices Based of information provided during time of tender"

OPTIONAL PRICING - NOT INCLUDED IN PC SUM	
Concrete Kerb to Driveway - no detail provided 62 lm @ $175.00	$10,850.00
Prep the underside of the exposed concrete driveway 150mm AP40, 211m2 @ $22.00	$4,642.00
Prepare and sow grass 1 LS @ $4,500.00	$4,500.00
TOTAL PC SUM	$19,992.00

213

FOUNDATION BLOCKWORK & FLOOR GROUND LEVEL

At the end of each month you will be issued a payment claim which generates a monthly figure that reflects the percentage of work completed for the month. This figure covers labour/ materials and subtrade invoices for the month. You will be issued your payment claim sheet, an invoice and your detailed payment tracker that records every penny you spend and how much you have left to pay.

Your payment terms are outlined in your contract. We ask that you read this carefully and adhere to the terms as we heavily rely on prompt payment to deliver you the best service possible.

If you ever have a problem with payments please contact us ASAP.

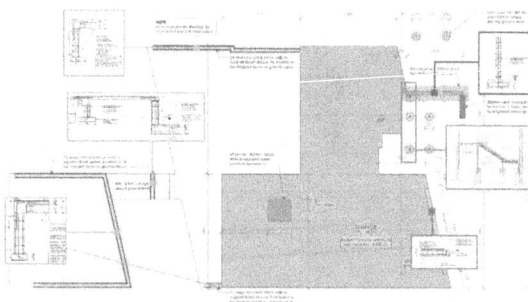

- 250mm thick slab with two layers (top and bottom) of HD16 @ 200 centres.
- 25 series concrete block walls reinforced with H16 at 200mm vertical centres and H12 and 400mm horizontal centres. Block wall supported by a 800mm wide footing to support ribraft above, foundation to be stepped down as ground slopes. 25 mpa concrete.
- 800mm wide x 200mm thick foundation supporting 20 Series block wing wall reinforced with H16 at 200mm vertical centres and H12 and 400mm horizontal centres..
- 300mm wide foundation to bottom of steps.
- Lift pit min. 300mm deep, reinforced with H16 @ 400mm centres each way.
- 450mm dia piles down to 400mm below existing ground level.

WATERPROOFING

Nuraply 3 part tanking membrane, protected by Nuralite protection board. Novaflow installed to the base of the block walls and backfilled with free draining granules. We have upgraded the waterproofing spec to wrap under the ground floor garage floor slab and the above Maxraft floor dpm to eliminate any weak points. Waterproofing is to the extent of highlighted areas in the two opposite pictured details.

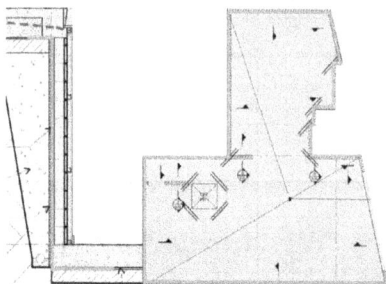

9. Present Your Quote in a Meeting as an Action Plan.

I like to think of this as setting the vibe. It's not just a quote, like, "Here's the price, bang, see you later." It's a really important and structured process, so allow about an hour for every presentation. The key thing is to know your quote in-depth. Spend a good amount of time studying the quote so that when questions come up, you can answer them quickly and accurately.

- When you present the quote, you've got to have the right people doing the right jobs at the right time. Have every part of the journey mapped out for future reference—from the information people get before coming to your office to what they can expect in the cover letter. It's all about sales choreography:

- Make sure your prospect knows exactly where to park. Then, when they come to the office, make sure they are received into the office by the office manager. The office manager should know exactly how to greet them.

- When they wait down in the foyer for a couple of minutes, ask them if they want water or a cappuccino. If you can share anything during that time, whether it's a bit of food or a cup of coffee, it's a great rapport builder.

When they're shown into the boardroom, seat them so they have a clear view of any indicators of your success, such as your Master Builder Awards.

Make sure both decision-makers are there. You can't go through a 40-60-minute presentation and then expect whoever's listening to it to go back and give that same information to their business partner or spouse.

If just one of them shows up quite often, they'll use that as an opportunity to stall: "Hey, well, I need to talk to my partner (or wife, fiancé, friend, dog, or whatever)." You want to avoid that. Also, if the person's significant other isn't involved in the decision-making process, they can feel left out and might resent it, so they'll push back no matter how good the proposal is. They're just pushing back because they weren't involved in it. Sometimes, they haven't talked about these things together, so you actually end up bringing things to light that will help move things along now that they're being talked about in front of you.

One of the key things is to give them *just* enough information. Don't give them information like "You've got 25 lengths of 3x2." I've seen some people's quotes that itemise every little bit of material on it and prices. That makes it very easy for someone to take that to another builder, get a price comparison and maybe come back with, "Actually, I can do those 30 cents a metre cheaper," or whatever it may be. So, if you give them too much information, it's too easy for them to get a comparable quote. It's better to have it broken down into larger sections, like "Structure," which might include all the windows. It should be big lump sums. So, if someone then says, "Hey, how much for your windows?" You can actually pull your window quote out from Rylock,[4] or whoever you use, and say, "It's $15,000." They go, "That's pretty reasonable." This is only if they ask.

If you do it in big sections like that, all your profit, markups, and overhead recoveries can be placed throughout the whole quote. We find that at the end of the day, the bottom figure is what's going to get them over the line, plus educating them on your process, project management, payment schedule, communication, and guarantee.

WINS FROM MEMBERS

DANIEL L. – SIX MONTHS IN WITH TPB

- *Before PBR was $40-$50 per hour. Now it's $118.*
- *He's now quoting and winning jobs 100% bigger than before (from $500k jobs to $1Million jobs)*
- *Converting leads at 50%*

---

[4] A windows and doors specialist in New Zealand.

- *Major confidence boost now that he understands the numbers much better*
- *Last job on Buildertrend all his job metrics were green (labour, time, COS, etc.)*

WAYDE M.

- *On track to 2x revenue this year. He has already earned 100% of 2023 revenue, year to date.*
- *Secrets to success: moving to design-build (closing more deals) and providing maximum value to leads (speed to lead and add tons of value)*

STEWART G.

- *About to lock in $990k + $1.4 million + $880k projects all at a minimum of 25% margins, with three more jobs being quoted in the pipeline.*
- *Business is growing well and slowly scaling up the team.*

10. Close the Deal, Receive the Deposit, and Sign the Contract

What generally happens when you're sitting at the table is that you'll have your front page on your quote, and it's got the breakdown. It has the final figure. So, the first thing they see is $100,000, $300,000, $1,000,000, or whatever it happens to be. So, very quickly, they'll look at that. That's where they make their first decision on it. Don't let them sit on that page too long. Be like, "Okay, this next page shows the…" And then go through the whole process. Basically, line by line, read the whole quote through. You can have your QS/estimator do that, and then you can pop in with the benefits, really painting the picture of what the finished product will be:

"Oh, wow. Imagine that room being done. It's going to be awesome."

Some people just look at the page of writing and the numbers, and they are happy with that. Make sure everything is proofread and looks professional.

One of the benefits of working with over 2500 building company owners is that we identify members who are using world-class best practices and getting great results in a specific area of their business. We then interview them, take their templates and systems (with their permission of course) and white label each asset for the whole community to use.

A rising tide lifts all boats. This is how our members are able to improve their results quickly with plug-and-play best practices of what's working right now. Our members use a high-converting Quote/Action Plan that allows them to win projects even when they charge 10%-20% higher than other builders.

Some people are more visual, so for them, have a set of plans showing how you're going to complete a certain stage of the build. The plans should be drawn out or illustrated digitally and highlighted in the areas you're going to talk about, complete with different colour filters of where the insulation is going or where the painting is starting and stopping, for example. The more visual the presentation and the more things you can talk about with confidence, the better. You should also have brochures from the suppliers you use for different aspects of the build if you don't have ones of whole existing builds that are similar to what theirs would be. Visuals add to your professionalism by improving your ability to go down to the details, and people like details. It makes something that can seem convoluted to them all very clear (specificity leads to credibility).

Other people are more kinesthetic—they want to touch and really *feel* things. For these folks, you want to have physical materials at the meeting. You might have a carpet sample. You might have a sample for a kwila[5] deck and one for a pine deck. Have as many bits and pieces lying around the table as you can, so you can talk about them and allow the prospect to really get a sense of what it would be like to be surrounded by these materials in their home.

[5] Tropical hardwood decking typically used in Australia and New Zealand

> *"After joining TPB, I got my charging for quotes process sorted out and finally have the confidence to ask for payment for quotes! I've spent years doing quotes for jobs that I was unlikely to get, and of course, doing them for no return. Also lost many a night and weekend pulling them together. Those days are over!"*
>
> —Alan M, Forfar

All the way through the meeting, assume you've got the job. Never sit there like you haven't got it. Just presume you've got it. You've done all the preliminary work; you can act as if you've got that job. So, future pace the conversation with the home owner like, "Oh yeah, when we turn up here, we'll do this and that. And we had a look at your site, and we think we'll put the toilet down that side, so the kids can still get the bikes out." The whole way through, it's your job already. It's their job to lose, not your job to get.

Price Factors That Are Out of Your Control

When you're doing your sales, it's best to be transparent with it all, including price rises and material delays. Things like this are not on you, so the client should know that this is just how it is. Even if it's a fixed-price contract, there should be a clause in the contract protecting you and the client (rise and fall clause).

ACTION STEPS

1. Download and implement the 10-Step Sales Process, including scripts, email questionnaire, WOW info pack, prelim budget, and action plan.

2. Start to charge for your expertise and time using the Prelim Budget Process.

3. Use a high converting quote/action plan to win more jobs at a higher profit margin consistently.

Scan the code for all the resources

MEMBER PROFILE: LEON G.

We inspected Leon's sales and marketing process and found the biggest opportunity was for him to start charging for his quotes (Prelim Budget Process) and valuable skills and time.

He would spend 30 hours drafting plans and letting prospects pick his brain, only to get 'no' for an answer. He was sick and tired of getting burned by prospects who used him as a price check with other builders.

They would come up with excuses like, "Your price is too high" or, "The other guy could start right away."

Deep down, he wanted to get paid for his time and expertise, but at the same time, he thought he couldn't charge for quotes because he needed to get his business going better. Other building companies offer free quotes, so he thought charging for them would scare away his prospects.

But in reality, it could help eliminate time wasters and people who've got an unrealistic scope of work versus their budget.

So, to get Leon paid for his quotes, we helped him dial in his scripting at the end of the site visit. In a nutshell, Leon offers his prospects a professional estimate, which includes a detailed timeline, an accurate budget, and a bound booklet. If they decide to walk away, he still gets paid for his time. But if they say yes, it gets absorbed into the contract. To make this work, we ensured the other moving pieces of his sales process were in place, including his info pack, website, and qualifying process.

These steps help Leon position himself as the builder of choice and build trust with his prospects. When he implemented the process, he got paid for 7 quotes at $3.5K each and signed all of them with margins above 20%.

This process-driven approach lets Leon get paid for his expertise and secure jobs at a higher margin.

CHAPTER 8 – SUMMARY
SET YOUR BUSINESS UP FOR SALE

What is the end goal of your business?

Is it to set it up for sale?

Do you hire a General Manager and work 3 – 4 days per week?

Do you structure a buy in with one of your team?

Or something else?

- Find out how much your business is worth now using the Biz Value Calculator and what it could be worth in 12 months with the right systems, strategies and team in place.

- Why partnerships fail and how to set yourself up for success.

- The 5 Step Process for Structuring a Buy In.

- Get the Builder's Buy In Checklist.

SET YOUR BUSINESS UP FOR SALE

The most important thing for the profitable building business owner to consider is what the end goal of their business is. What's your Business Maturity Date (BMD)? What are you working towards?

If you want to always own 100% of your business, netting $500,000, working four days a week, that's perfectly fine. But I'm here to show you there are options other than this that might be more fulfilling for you.

You can sell your business two to five years from now, go and start doing spec builds, start a scaffolding/joinery business, or just work in your business half the time with enough cash flow from it so you can focus on creating true wealth for yourself. To make any of these scenarios work and come out of them profitable, you could consider bringing a partner on board and structuring a buy-in. Or set the business up for sale and ensure that you maximise your asset value and sale price.

A buy-in is where you sell part of your business to an incoming partner—they "buy in" to your business. It might be someone in your business, like a project manager or a foreman, or it could be someone external to your business, like an investor. Here are some reasons why you might want to bring in a partner:

- You need money.

- You want to retain key staff.

- You are nearing retirement age.

- You've got other business opportunities you want to go off and pursue, like developments, scaffolding, or importing materials.

- You haven't got your core business running smoothly enough, so you really want to tie someone in and have that right-hand man by your side to give you the comfort of continuity in your business.

- You want to exit your business, and the buy-in is part of your succession planning whereby you're going to bring someone on board who's going to buy 100% of your business over a certain period of time, and you need to decide how much you want to vest, and over what period of time.

In this chapter, I'm going to give you some things to consider if structuring a buy-in sounds like something you want to do. Secondly, I'm going to give you a 5-step process you can use to make this buy-in happen for you, along with some tools to assist along the way.

> *"Marti helped me build my marketing funnel, and I'm fully booked for the next year. This week alone, I got four paid quotes and signed all four of them. Not having to worry about finding the next job allowed me to focus on more important tasks and grow the business."*
>
> –Ricki C, Tauranga

Before we talk about how to structure a buy-in, let's run some figures to show you how to determine whether having a buy-in would help or hurt your profit (remember, we don't fear numbers anymore based on what we've learned in *The Profitable Builder*, right?).

IS A BUY-IN WORTH IT FOR YOU?

The biggest thing to consider is how structuring a buy-in will affect your profit. If, for example, you're currently doing $3 million in revenue and you're certain that you'll get to your $4 million target in the next 18 months, then why would you want to sell part of that? Could you achieve that same result with your project manager as an employee, as opposed to the opportunity cost of selling them 20%, 33%, or 50% of your business?

On the other hand…let's say your gross margin is at 15% on $2 million. That gives you a gross profit of $300,000. Let's say your fixed costs are $200,000, which gives you a net profit of $100,000. If your business hasn't been well systemised, you might have a price-earnings ratio[1] of 1.5.

Let's say your company is worth $150,000, plus stock (at cost) and assets (at book value). If you were to sell a third of that to a project manager or someone coming into your business, your return will be $50,000. You're going to get $50,000 back for your 10 years of work, and you now only own 67% of the business, and they own 33% of it.

If you can now get from $2 million in revenue to $5 million over the next one to two years, and you increase your gross margin from 15% to 20%, you'll have a gross profit of $1 million. Your fixed costs will need to increase to sustain that $5 million revenue. So you might need a project manager, a QS/estimator, a full-time office person, or maybe a part-time marketer. If you've got fixed costs of $500,000 from your $1 million gross profit, it means you have a net profit of $500,000. If you've put the right systems into your business, this will help increase your multiple from 1.5 to between 3 and 4[2]. Many of the members we've assisted in preparing their businesses for sale have successfully sold them for a multiple between 3 and 4.

---

[1] The amount an investor invests in a company to get $1, also known as PE ratio or price-earnings multiple.

[2] For a small to medium-sized enterprise (SME), a typical price to earning ratio is 1X to 4X. For a franchise, it can range from 4X to 10X.

So, if you've got $500,000 net profit and a multiple price-earnings ratio of 3, your business has now gone from being worth $100,000 plus stock and assets, to $1.5 million plus stock and assets.

Company Valuation

	Now	2 Years
Revenue	$2M	$5M
Gross Margin	15%	20%
Gross Profit	$300,000	$1,000,000
Fixed Costs	$200,000	$500,000
Net Profit	$100,000	$500,000
P/E Ratio	1.5	3
Stock @ Cost	–	–
Assets @ book value	–	–
Company Value (& Stock & Assets)	$150,000	$1.5M

THE MOMENT OF TRUTH

What you have to weigh up is whether that person's 33%, which they paid $50,000 for, helped you get to that result. Ultimately, the sale actually cost you $450,000 because their $50,000 is now worth $500,000. Good win for them. Maybe not as good for you as the business owner.

So, in this scenario, you would ask yourself three key questions:

1. Is getting their contribution worth it for me?

2. What real-world value will they bring?

3. Am I willing to give up that opportunity cost?

Most importantly, could you have gotten this profit without them? If the answer is no, then structuring a buy-in will actually help you become a more profitable building company, thus helping to make your dreams and goals a reality (and reducing the weight of having all of the decisions solely on your shoulders).

BUILDER'S ROADMAP TIP:

IF YOU'RE NOT READY TO GO ALL-IN, CONSIDER A PROFIT SHARE INSTEAD.

You can offer profit shares to your employees as incentives based directly on their performance. This option means less commitment, fewer long-term implications, and less complexity. This doesn't qualify as a buy-in, but rather it's the precursor to it that you can use as an option if you're not ready to do a full-blown partnership with someone else, in which they buy a part of your business.

If you've determined that a buy-in *would* boost your profitability and help you accomplish your business and life goals, let's start by talking about some common problems that can pop up and how to avoid them.

WHY PARTNERSHIPS FAIL

In terms of priorities, where are you focused? Are you as focused on the business as the new person coming in is expecting?

Typically what happens between new partners is that there are different expectations of the workload. So, it's very critical that you clarify exactly what each party is going to do. This is why job descriptions are so important. You need to clearly state the following from the beginning: each person's role, tasks, and hours they're going to put in are; how much they're going to be paid; and their scorecard with KPIs and KPAs.

I had a friend who had a business, and he had three partners in the business. They all had job descriptions. One partner had put $600,000 in to start the business, and one of the partners also owned another business, a web development business, and he wasn't performing. They gave him opportunities to get more leads and sales because they wanted him to perform, but he wasn't hitting his KPIs. They determined that if the business wasn't hitting these KPIs, they would have to decide if the person in charge of those KPIs should have their shares bought back off them, which is indeed what happened. A scenario like this is something you should prepare for by creating a process for it.

Another thing that can be detrimental to a partnership is foul play. To prevent anything sketchy from going on, make sure there is some form of protection in your partnership, or at least document everything so that if anything does happen, you can recover any losses you may have had. It's important that both parties know it's normal to take precautions, and it shouldn't affect the relationship in any way. I once had a business partner in a pet store we owned 50/50 who was acting as if it was still his own personal bank account. Needless to say, this didn't end well. Lawyers got involved, and it was a protracted and stressful nine months to get my initial investment back.

Other common reasons a lot of partnerships fail are:

- A lack of clear business goals

- A lack of performance criteria and milestones as you're growing

- Not having a clear plan of action, with clear KPIs and monthly and quarterly reviews to make sure you're on track.

It is vital to address these steps from the start. However, before you bring on a business partner, be sure to weigh all of the pros and cons. Then if it makes sense for you, then you can proceed.

BUILDER'S ROADMAP TIP:

CHOOSE SOMEONE YOU TRUST WHOSE SKILLS COMPLEMENT YOURS.

For a partnership to really work, make sure you both have complementary skill sets. There's no point in you both being great at sales or you both being great at project management. You need different skills that complement each other. One person might be great at the project management side of things, working with the guys on-site, sales, and working with clients. Whilst the other person might be great at pricing and contract administration. Complementary skill sets are essential for partners to have in order for things to go smoothly and for there to be no blind spots in how the business is managed.

THE 5-STEP PROCESS FOR STRUCTURING A BUY-IN

Step 1: Get Clear on Ownership and How It's Managed

What is each party bringing to the table? Whose name is going to be on the business? The following are things to consider on the part of the purchaser for new ownership, depending on the type of buy-in you have going on:

If you're only going to be involved in the business 50%, is it still going to have your name on it? For example, in Bakers Builds, Auckland, New Zealand, a new owner bought 75% of the business but decided to continue using the original business name.

Does the purchaser want to simply be a shareholder in the company that has your name on it, or do they want to change the name to reflect the new type of ownership you are pursuing? Will it now become Auckland Premium Homes?

What is the mindset of the purchaser going into this situation? When it comes to purchasers who are employees—thinking they are buying in to maybe ride on the coat tails of an entrepreneur who has been doing the hard yards and setting all the foundations for success—are they prepared as the buyer to be that hard-charging, motivated person now that you're potentially less engaged, off doing other ventures like a second business or developments?

These are all big things to think about when you're looking at going into a partnership with someone. These are things they will be thinking about or need to think about to be clear on what their commitment level is.

Have a meeting with your potential business partner and figure out:

- What are their goals?

- What do they want out of the partnership in 12 months, 3 years, and beyond?

- What is their vision for the business?

- What is their family and life vision?

This might sound very personal, but you need to understand the person who is going to own part of your business. You can ask them these questions directly or just listen to what they're saying to answer the following questions for yourself:

1. What are their expectations of the job?

2. What are they expecting from you?

3. What are their goals for themselves?

4. What are their goals for the business?

5. Where do they see the business heading?

And what about you, the vendor? What's your mindset? How engaged will you be in the primary business? Or are you going to be off doing something else?

What if it Doesn't Work?

Work out in advance what should happen if someone wants to leave. For example, if either party leaves to start another building company, there might be a non-compete clause. Or, if the partner is an employee and they get a job somewhere else, deciding whether or not they can still be a shareholder is extremely important. There needs to be a clear exit strategy for both parties.

Also, work out what happens if it doesn't work. What if the relationship doesn't work? Do you still want to stay friends? How does that work upon exiting? And what if the business itself doesn't work? You might have to work out whether more capital should be put into the business should this happen. Does this then dilute one person's equity if they can't afford to put in their share of the money required?

In terms of managing this partnership, you'll need to have regular meetings, whether they be weekly, monthly, or quarterly. During these meetings, clarify roles and expectations, and include KPIs attached to the KPAs associated with each role defined in your job descriptions and scorecards. Know and show your numbers to make sure that you're on track. Getting everything in writing is also incredibly important—from contracts and shareholder agreements to meeting notes.[3]

Now, remember that you're going from having your name on the company—it's been your way or the highway thus far—to having an incoming person with ownership in the company. How will you handle this? You both need to be aligned from the start with a clear vision, clear goals, and clear expectations.

---

[3] Meeting notes are super important so that if things go pear shaped, you can always look back on those meeting notes and say, "Well, you said you would do this. We agreed that we would run the business this way."

When you have a partner, you'll have to remember it's no longer just your business. You can't unilaterally decide, "We're going to go and do a retreat in Fiji and take the whole team." You have to consult with your business partner because you're now accountable to them as your co-owner.

It's important for you to determine exactly how decisions will be made. You might need quorums[4] for meetings. And in terms of spending, are you going to have a limit? Anything over $1000 (or $10,000) might need two signatories—both of you will have to decide if you're actually going to go through with a large purchase or hire that new team member.

BUILDER'S ROADMAP TIP:

GET CLEAR ON WAYS THE BUSINESS WILL CHANGE WITH A BUY-IN.

When it comes to a new partnership, you or your partner may have some ideas for expansion you will have to take into account. For example, there may be a different location or different types of builds that are added to the existing business. There may be a different market you and/or your partner have in mind that will work best for the new partnership. For example, one of our Boardroom members, Richard Phiskie of Dimension Building in Timaru, opened a second South Island location in Twizel. Another member, Brendon Sowerby from Next Level Construction in Auckland, opened a joinery business with a partner.

Many of our members will add another build type and look at a different company setup for:

- New builds
- Renovations
- Passive Homes

---

[4] A minimum number of people that should be present.

You may also need a new website, case studies, marketing, info pack, pricing process, team on-site, alliance with architects, or design and build process.

Extra Builder's Roadmap Tip: Do thorough research before saying yes to anything!

Step 2: Pick Your Percentages and Work Out the Specifics

Next, decide what percentage you want to sell and over what period of time. Is it 10%, 20%, 25%, 33%, or 50%, and is there the opportunity for this person to buy more as time progresses? Will the business have to hit certain goals? For example, I sold 25% of my business to my General Manager, Owen, with the stipulation that if we hit our 12-month profit goal, he could exercise the option to purchase a further 8%, taking him to 33%.

Also, what entity, or entities, are they buying into? Are they just buying into the overarching building company, or are they also buying what's within that entity? Are they also buying, for example, the retaining wall business within that entity? They might also consider buying into any future aspects of what that business does. If the business starts a separate division doing house and land packages.

VENDOR FINANCE

It's also important to decide whether you're leaving any money in for the partner to pay back, which is known as vendor finance. For example, let's say you decided that for your 33% of the business, they were going to pay $100,000. They might stump up $25,000 at first and pay off the remaining $75,000 over the next 18 months. You could have them pay that back out of profit share or actual cash—it can be done any way you want to structure it as long as it's clear, makes sense, is documented, and is agreed upon by both parties.

Additionally, consider if there's going to be sweat equity, which means they can earn equity simply by maybe taking a lower operating salary, thus paying back more. So, instead of them getting a salary of $125,000, including their bonus for being a great project manager (if that's who you're going into this partnership with), they might only be paid $70,000, and the remaining $55,000 goes towards paying down their equity.

Work out the logistics of all of this. If they are paying $100,000 for their share, do you require them to have $25,000 in cash that they put in for their share of the business, or do you need $50,000 to start? Whatever you do, get some form of commitment so they have skin in the game; ideally, they should be putting some money into the business right away to show that.

BUILDER'S ROADMAP TIP:

CAREFULLY PLAN AND COMMUNICATE YOUR DIVIDEND POLICY.[5]

This isn't optional—you need to put a dividend policy in place. The top aspect of this here is to make sure it's a policy that works for your profitability and operational cashflow requirements to run the business day to day.

An example of a dividend policy would be where you retain 50% of the profits (after tax) for your operating budget and then distribute the other 50% each month or 90 days in arrears for the previous month/quarter. Let's say you made $400,000 profit (after tax) during the year. You might decide to keep $200,000 to go towards the operating budget and the other $200,000 you distribute $50,000 each quarter pro rata[6] at the shareholding ratios of the two partners.

---

[5] Your company's plan for paying out dividends.
[6] Proportionally in ratio of the equity partner's shareholding percentage.

Step 3: Decide how the business will be valued.

The next step is working out the valuation process—how the business will be valued. A business is valued based on 3 components:

1. **Stock at cost:** The value of your materials and any other products used for the construction of each project.

2. **Assets at book value:** This includes your computers, tools, vehicles, and website at the depreciated book value. So, for example, whether you're using straight-line depreciation[7] or scaled depreciation, you'll figure out how much those assets are each worth. A computer that's three years old, for example, might only be worth $200.

3. **Goodwill:** Goodwill is the difference between the net tangible asset backing[8] and the sale price you ask for the business (or that someone pays). As an example, if your stock and assets are worth $100,000—that's the net tangible asset backing. If you had a sale price of $700,000 for your business, then the difference is $600,000, which is the goodwill.

Now, if your price-earnings ratio was three, this means you would have a net profit of $200,000. So $200,000 X 3 gives you your goodwill value of $600,000.

The price-earnings multiple (PE ratio) relates to how likely the financial result you got in the previous year, or the current financial period, will be replicated. The higher the multiple, the more likely it is that you'll be able to replicate that financial result.[9] Remember that most small to medium

---

[7] This type of depreciation divides the cost of the asset equitably across the time it is used.

[8] These are the net tangible assets that allow the business to run their day-to-day operations.

[9] Franchises tend to be better systemised, so there's more chance of being able to replicate the result. A higher price-earnings ratio would depend on how well systemised and documented your processes are, how good your marketing is and how good your sales process is. How much forward work have you got booked in? What margin are you getting your jobs at? How good is your project management? And are key staff going to stay on after the sale date (or the transition of the business)? Refer back to the tools in *The Profitable Builder* to increase your multiple.

enterprises (SMEs), especially building companies because they're not usually that well systemized, will have a price-earnings ratio between one and four.

You should always get two accountants to value a business and then typically take the average between the two. So, find two great accountants, agree on a valuation process, and provide supporting documentation for the valuation. How long this takes depends on how big your business is and how quickly you want to get this done.

> *"I never thought I would be drafting a buy-in opportunity for an investor with an immense business acumen. I was able to fly to California for a personal event, and when I came back, everything was running smoothly. It would've taken me more years to achieve all of these without Marti's help."*
>
> —Elk G, Texas

Step 4: Work Out What to Do About Your Intellectual Property

If you're bringing the intellectual property you developed over the last 10 years, you have a few options depending on your situation:

- You can gift it to the company
- You can include it as part of the sale price
- You can license it (for $1 or whatever price you agree upon) and have it in a separate holding company[10]

---

[10] I would recommend this option, but make sure you get professional advice based on your specific situation. Having that intellectual property in a holding company allows you to then go and do that over and over again, should you want to with other team members or in different locations and businesses.

Step 5: A Systematic Approach to Buy-Ins Using the Right Paperwork

At this point, it's time to structure your business plan for how you're going to realise a successful buy-in. This business plan will include your KPAs, your strategies, your SWOT analysis,[11] and your finances. It would also include your targets on a one-page dashboard.

The next key thing you need is a shareholder agreement between both shareholders that describes what each person is going to do and how the company will operate. Here are some important clauses that should be included:

- **Valuation process upon sale:** This might actually be different to the valuation process upon purchase. It may mean that you have a different way of valuing it or that you have different accountants value it. Whatever you both decide on needs to be in the contract. A good practice is to have the company valued each year.

- **A buy-sell provision:** This means that if you want to sell the business, the other shareholder might have the first and/or last right of refusal. This means they get the opportunity to buy it—either the first chance to buy it and/or the last chance to buy it.

- **An insurance clause within the buy-sell provision:** This clause ensures that if something were to happen to you and you passed away, your business partner wouldn't end up in business with your spouse (which he may or may not want to do.) So, in this situation, the insurance policy that's funded by the company would pay out your spouse for the shares that you own in the business at the valuation that you've agreed upon. That means that your business partner would then own 100% of the business and your family gets paid the agreed upon value.

---

[11] This acronym stands for Strengths, Weaknesses, Opportunities, and Threats.

- **A tag and drag clause:** Let's say you were the 75% shareholder in a business (you sold 25% of it), and someone came along and said they wanted to buy your building company. This means that you can force the minority shareholder (the one who only owns 25%) to sell with you to the new purchaser.

- **Securities and personal guarantees clause:** If the bank has security over your house (or your farm if you're from the country), this clause will determine whether those personal guarantees will be released upon the new person coming on board or if the new person will get added onto the security register.

Include whatever you both agree is going to make it work in a shareholder agreement. Get everything down on paper, make it clear in both people's minds, and make sure that you have great communication, weekly meetings, monthly budget reviews, and quarterly planning to build a great business together.

BUILDER'S ROADMAP TIP:

CONSIDER A PROFIT SHARE/BUY-IN COMBO: THE PLAN B.

The plan B type of buy-in is the best of both worlds. This has been used by many of our members, and it allows you to:

- retain your existing team members.
- test drive being in business together for 12-18 months.
- give them a great opportunity to own their own business.
- systemise your core business along the way and increase the value of the company.

The way you do this is that you first agree that you're going to set up a new business with the potential purchaser, who is your employee—let's say it's your project manager. First you focus on the core business you already have. Set up a Business Maturity Date (BMD) for the next 12 or 18 months for the core business from the time you decide this, and incentivise the potential purchaser to hit the KPIs to make this a reality. This way, when your core business hits that maturity date—let's say this means that it goes from revenue of $2 million to $5 million and the gross profit margin grows from 17% to 22%—you and the purchaser go and start the new business with some of the profit that's been achieved. This gives you a definite date and that certainty you need to make this happen successfully together.

With the new business, agree on the percentages each person will go into the business at. If it's 50/50, you're both equally committed to the new business.

The great thing about this is you retain 100% of your existing core business!

GET YOUR BUILDER'S BUY-IN CHECKLIST

This is a lot, I know. We have a checklist we've put together to help you not only decide if this is for you, but also to see what options you have that are specific to your situation.

It will also help you determine who would be good in your business to potentially do this with. Using this checklist, you can also decide how much you want to sell/divest—whether it's 10%, 25%, or 33%—and whether you want to do it as a bonus, profit share, equity, or plan B with a new business. You'll use your Business Maturity Date to determine this and then go through the documents we have attached to the checklist: your shareholder agreement, a document for the valuation of your business, and your one-page plan.

We're happy to help you see how all of this could benefit your company and help you take it to the next level.

ACTION STEPS

1. Decide if it makes sense to bring on a business partner.

2. Choose the best option for you and them:

- Profit Share

- Shareholding Equity partner

- Plan B (18-month test drive and then set up a new company split 50/50)

3. Go through the provided training and checklist on The Systematic Approach to Buy-Ins.

Scan the code for all the resources:

CONCLUSION

We've covered a lot of ground in this book.

In your hands you hold the tools and knowledge to create your ideal life by building a great business. One that gives you true wealth – both more money AND more time.

The transition from business 'operator' to 'owner' starts with a mindset shift to get off the "Builders' Hamster Wheel" and create a business worth owning.

A Profitable Builder focuses on systems onsite and in the office to go from chaos to control.

A Profitable Builder hires, trains and builds a great team, so they can work on the business, instead of IN it all the time.

A Profitable Builder prices to a target margin of at least 20% plus and improves profit on each project using the 9 margin levers.

In order to get better results, something needs to change. If you continue doing the same things, you will continue to get the same results.

THE FORMULA FOR CHANGE:

$D \times V + FS \geq R$ is your catalyst for change.

The Change Formula

$$(D \times V) + FS > R$$

Dissatisfaction x Vision + First Steps > Resistance

To build a better business and buy back your time, it all starts with what are you unhappy or frustrated with in your business?

DISSATISFACTION — IF YOU'VE FOUND YOURSELF THINKING:

- There has to be a better way
- I'm going around in circles
- Why aren't I making more profit?
- Is this as good as it gets?

All progress starts with the truth.

Looking at the man in the mirror and saying – "I'm capable of more" and "I deserve better."

VISION

Then it's getting clear on what does success look like – both personally and professionally.

Every house starts with a set of plans of what it looks like when it's finished.

What type of business do I want to own?

This is what to get clear on with your BMD – Business Maturity Date.

- How much profit are you making each year?
- What revenue do I need to hit?
- How many projects do you want to do and how big are they?
- What role do you play in the business?

AND more importantly, what do I NOT do?

- Is it pricing projects?

- When is your last day of pricing and whom will you hire to do it?

Clarity on what you are building leads to it being more concrete and achievable to hit your milestones as you take action towards your goals

Then reverse engineer the steps needed to hit each goal.

- Business Maturity Date (what success looks like)
- 90 Day Plan to get there with specific strategies for your situation
- Personal Goals Vision Book (the fuel, motivation and rewards)

FIRST STEPS

So if one of your goals is to get back one day per week, then to find those 8 hours, we go through the PBR (Professional Builder's Rate) exercise:

- Stop Doing List
- Freedom Finder
- Fun/Skills Matrix, and then
- Perfect Week/Default Diary to build out your week so it sets you up for success

Now you are now focussed on the 80/20 needle movers that make the biggest difference in your business.

These activities should be in your Genius Zone:

- You love doing them
- You are naturally great at them
- They make a big difference to the business

RESISTANCE

You may be thinking . . . if it was this easy, I would have done it already.

The Builders' Blueprint Roadmap for becoming a Profitable Builder is simple but <u>not</u> easy.

That's because it includes two key steps to progress forward . . .

You can't grow past your identity and this needs to level up as you climb each rung of the Builder's Ladder.

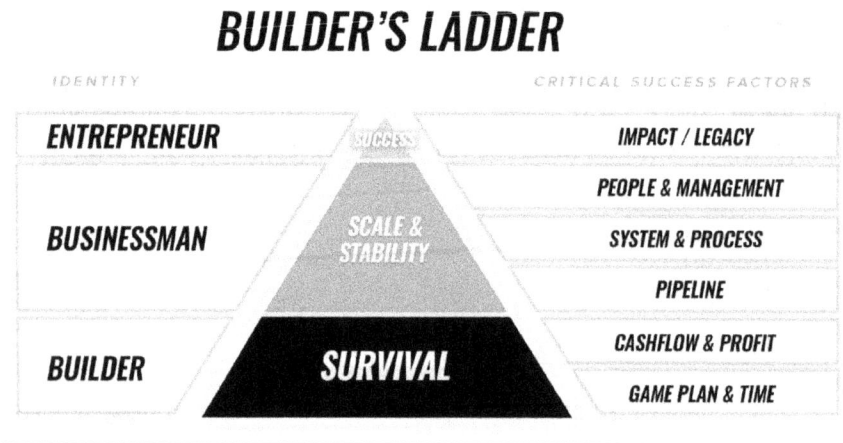

BUILDER'S LADDER

IDENTITY   CRITICAL SUCCESS FACTORS

ENTREPRENEUR	SUCCESS	IMPACT / LEGACY
		PEOPLE & MANAGEMENT
BUSINESSMAN	SCALE & STABILITY	SYSTEM & PROCESS
		PIPELINE
		CASHFLOW & PROFIT
BUILDER	SURVIVAL	GAME PLAN & TIME

These transitions typically happen between from Builder to Business Owner $1 – 2m as you step off the tools and then at $7m - $10m as you build out your management team and need to grow your leadership skills to get things done through other people.

The second is to break any self-limiting beliefs that keep you stuck at each level.

- Clients only want to deal with me
- I can't be off-site or things turn to custard
- This is a 10% town… no one charges any higher

- I can't trust anyone else to price work

- I can't charge for quotes or I won't win any jobs

- I can't find good people

These limiting beliefs will keep you stuck in your current situation.

"Playing small" doesn't serve you, your family, your team or your clients.

Playing a bigger game allows you to fulfill your potential and achieve your business and life's goals.

Overcoming these <u>limiting beliefs</u> and upgrading your identify can be done by:

- Being in the right environment; around a community of other business owners who are on the same journey as you.

- People one to two steps ahead who have solved the challenges you may currently be going through and can shed light on the path ahead and which pot holes to avoid.

- And, those "North Star" business owners who have achieved what you want to achieve and can provide inspiration, motivation and coaching to help you get there faster.

TAKE MASSIVE ACTION

Over the last twenty years I've noticed in our mastermind and coaching programmes the people who win the most are:

- Not the smartest (they often get in their own way and over-think things and experience "paralysis by analysis")

- It's the action takers who get shit done

CONCLUSION

Take massive action towards your goals.

As General Patton said, "A good plan, violently executed right now, is better than the perfect plan next week".

All the information and strategies covered in this book are worthless if you don't take action!

To know and not do, is the same as not knowing at all. If you continue doing what you've always done, you will get what you've always got!

Take action right now to build a better business.

1. Download the $3000 Builder's Ultimate Bundle . . .

2. Take the Health Audit . . .

3. Book your complimentary coaching call and see what's possible for your business

Here's to your success,

Marti Amos

WANT TO TAKE YOUR BUSINESS TO THE NEXT LEVEL?

I have three questions to ask you:

1. What difference would it make for you in the next 90 days to get those headaches on-site ironed out?

2. How would it feel to have a productive team and an extra $50,000 or $250,000 sitting in the bank with fewer calls to go on-site to put out fires?

3. What difference would it make to have more client success and more peace of mind because you've got the right systems running your business?

We give you the step-by-step processes along with all the systems to make this a reality. We then check in with you each week to see if you need help and make sure you're on track. Becoming a part of the Professional Builder team has helped so many building company owners create more profit, all whilst minimising their stress and buying back their nights and weekends.

> *"I went to Charleston with my wife. We went for a helicopter ride and jet skiing. We also hired two new project managers and our gross margin is still at 20%. Thanks to Marti and the TPB crew, we have systems that help us buy back our time and focus on helping our guys improve."*
>
> —Jason G, Charlotte NC

NEXT STEPS

NOT SURE WHERE TO START?

Book a free 1-1 coaching call with us.

First, we'll have a chat to see if we can actually help you. If we can, we'll schedule a game plan call where we will focus on three key areas:

1. Define what success looks like for you and your business in 12 months and beyond.

2. Map out specific strategies tailored to you, your situation and your business to help you achieve your goals.

3. Plug your numbers into the TPB Profit Planner to see how much extra money you can make and time you can save by implementing the right strategies.

Here's to your success. I look forward to hearing about your wins!

Book your call below:

PAY IT FORWARD

I've given you the best strategies that we have learned over the last 21 years growing building companies to help you take your business to the next level.

I've held nothing back to help you move your business forward with the systems and templates in this book.

If you believe I've accomplished my goal with this book and given you value, I'd ask you to 'pay it forward' and share it with someone who may benefit from it.

You can gift a downloadable copy to three friends. Just scan the QR code below, enter their names and details, and we'll send them a free copy of this book.

YOUR $3000 BUILDER'S BUSINESS BUNDLE

GET $3,000 WORTH
OF BUSINESS RESOURCES & COACHING

Builders Business Bundle: Get the full $3,000 Worth of Profit-Boosting, Business Growth Strategies. As a special bonus to help you grow your business, I'd like to offer you an incredible free gift – our exclusive "$3,000 Builders Business Bundle."

This bundle includes:

1. 11 Premium Resources (referenced throughout this book):

Templates, checklists, calculators, and more, covering every aspect of your business (valued at $1,500).

1. The Builders Roadmap
2. The Health Audit
3. Professional Builders Rate (PBR) Calculator
4. A-Z of Operations
5. Business Maturity Date (BMD) Calculator

6. 90 Day Business Plan
7. 4 Financial Levers Calculator
8. 287 Point Quality Assurance Checklist
9. 1% referral system
10. 10-Step Sales Process
11. How to Structure a Buy- in Masterclass

2. Exclusive Members-Only Masterclass (valued at $500):

Get access to our members' area and watch the "How to Never Lose Money on a Construction Project" masterclass—practical strategies to protect your profit on every job.

3. One on One Game Plan Call (valued at $1000)::

Together, we'll take a deep dive into your business in terms of your sales & marketing, team & systems, and profit & cashflow to reveal where your biggest opportunities are.

From that, we'll identify the top 3-5 plug-n-play systems that will have the biggest and fastest impact on your results... and put them into a step-by-step "game plan" for you.

Then finally, we'll plug your numbers into our profit calculator to see how much extra money you can make (and how much time you can buy back).

You'll walk away with full confidence and clarity on what needs to happen over the next 90 days to reach your goals.

Visit www.profitablebuilderbook.com/resources or scan the QR code below to claim your bundle.

ABOUT THE AUTHOR

Marti Amos is an entrepreneur, business coach, author, podcaster and founder of The Professional Builder.

The Professional Builder helps contractors and residential building company owners build profitable companies with world class systems that produce true wealth - both more money AND more time.

Since 2004, Marti and TPB have helped thousands of company owners reclaim their sanity, build great businesses that are worth owning, with the right systems.

Marti is an avid traveller, massive petrol head, motorcyclist and 1980's heavy metal aficionado.

Marti lives in Auckland, New Zealand, with his wife Kelly, boys Zak and Ashton & Rocky the Rottweiler.

www.ingramcontent.com/pod-product-compliance
Lightning Source LLC
Chambersburg PA
CBHW061150220326
41599CB00025B/4428